T0088145

# OFFICIALLY OFF THE CLOCK

## BEST WISHES FOR A HAPPY RETIREMENT

ULYSSES PRESS

Published in the U.S. by:
ULYSSES PRESS
P.O. Box 3440
Berkeley, CA 94703
www.ulyssespress.com

ISBN: 978-1-64604-043-8
Library of Congress Control Number: 2020931855

Printed in Korea by Artin Printing Company through Four Colour Print Group
10 9 8 7 6 5 4 3 2 1

Acquisitions editor: Casie Vogel
Managing editor: Claire Chun
Editor: Renee Rutledge
Proofreader: Miriam Jones
Cover design: what!design @ whatweb.com
Cover photograph: © Javier Brosch/shutterstock.com
Interior design: Jake Flaherty
Interior photographs: © shutterstock.com; page 3 © Katrina Brown; page 6 © Olist; page 9 © Buy This; page 10, 46 © Monkey Business Images; page 13 © Masarik; page 14 © Istvan Csak; page 17, 45 © Javier Brosch; page 18 © Aleksey Boyko; page 21 © Masarik; page 22 © Monika Wisniewska; page 25 © Dan Smith Photography; page 26 © Sundays Photography; page 29 © KristinaSh; page 30 © Daniela Breznova; page 33 © Aneta Jungerova; page 34 © Kuznetsov Alexey; page 37 © Darina Matasova; page 38 © alexei_tm; page 41 © Linn Currie; page 42 © KikoStock; page 49 © Wasitt Hemwarapornchai; page 50 © Jolanta Beinarovica; page 53 © ValSN; page 54 © Tatiana Zinchenko; page 57 © PardoY; page 58 © StockMediaSeller; page 61 © Christine Wilson Photos; page 62 © mj-tim photography

Wishing You a Very Happy Retirement!

Congratulations! Say goodbye to the daily grind and get down to the real work: retirement.

It's your time to hit the golf course, soak up the sun, whip out your AARP card, enjoy those coveted senior discounts, and—of course—celebrate the best years of your life!

There are no more grumpy bosses to tell you what to do...

...instead it's your chance
to chart your own course!

No more carpal tunnel...

...more like carpe diem!

Stop dreaming about taking a nap at work...

...and start living
the dream!

Avoid the afternoon slump...

...and make every afternoon happy hour!

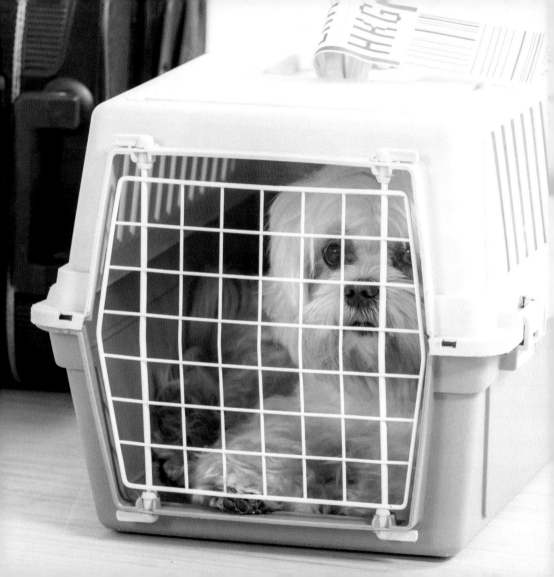

Stop feeling trapped
by work travel...

...and start feeling the
wind in your hair!

File away that frustrating paperwork...

...and open the next
chapter of your life!

Cut the cord on long conference calls...

...and dial in to fun!

Turn off boring busywork....

...and turn up the heat
on your hobbies!

# Hang up the hard hat...

...and pick up your nine iron!

Decline the invite
to another boring
office party...

# ...and RSVP to the party of your life!

# Put away those business suits...

...and put on your swimsuit!

Spend less time stuck
in bad meetings...

...and spend more time
with your loved ones!

Avoid stop-and-go traffic
on your commute...

...and stop and smell
the daisies instead!

# Finally, it's time to stop living to work...

...and start living your
best retired life!

## About the Author

**Rex Barkington** is a retired retriever and a very good boy. His hunting days are long behind him; in his retired life he is mostly focused on sniffing out treats. Rex spends his days napping on the golf course, napping by the pool, and napping on the beach. He lives in Florida.

# Contents

# Introduction

Xenofeminism, or XF, can to some extent be viewed as a labour of bricolage, synthesizing cyberfeminism, posthumanism, acceleration-ism, neorationalism, materialist feminism, and so on, in an attempt to forge a project suited to contemporary political conditions. From this litany of influences xenofeminism assembles, not a hybrid politics – which would suggest the prior existence of some impossible, un-hybridized state – but a politics without 'the infection of purity'.[1] In collecting, discarding, and revising existing perspectives – in stripping its myriad influences for parts – xenofeminism positions itself as a project for which the future remains open as a site of radical recomposition. This book is a first attempt at teasing out the underpinnings, arguments, and implications of 2015's xenofeminist manifesto in an extended form. However, it is important to note that this is just one interpretation of a polysemic project – a project riven with the unresolved tensions that come from collaboration across difference.

Each of the six members of Laboria Cuboniks – the xenofeminist working group of which I am a part – would likely emphasize different aspects of the manifesto, foregrounding some tendencies over others on account of our varied backgrounds, interests, and politics. The process of negotiating between our various feminist commitments has been one of the most satisfying and illuminating elements of our collective labour over the past three years. The manifesto remains a document that we are all happy to stand behind, and which we continue to incorporate into our individual practice – be that as musicians, artists, archaeologists, theorists, activists, coders, or poets. I would like to use this book to advance my own variation of XF, whilst continuing to acknowledge the divergent strands shaping the project as a whole. This is not *the* book on xenofeminism, then, but rather *a* book on xenofeminism.

I would like to start by briefly acknowledging some of the limits of this text, along with what I hope to achieve over the coming pages. *Xenofeminism* is not a thoroughgoing review of existing academic literature, and nor is it a lengthy monograph on feminist theories of science and technology. Rather, it is a polemic or a provocation – one grounded in a self-consciously idiosyncratic selection of critical material.[2] The references underpinning this text have been chosen not for their comprehensive articulation of the simultaneity of gender, technology, race, and sexualities, but for their suggestiveness and utility in terms of developing one particular strand of the XF project. The red thread uniting the chapters that follow represents what I consider to be one of the most compelling territories for any emerging xenofeminist position: reproduction, both biological and social. It is around this theme that the arguments of *Xenofeminism* converge.

Chapter 1 offers a partial definition of XF, sketching out some of the broad concepts that will ground subsequent chapters. In particular, the manifesto's treatment of three key ideas – technomaterialism, anti-naturalism, and gender abolitionism – will be explored, in order to indicate where they might contribute to a xenofeminist politics of reproduction. In Chapter 2, I turn to XF futurities – and, more precisely, to the need to develop visions of the future that are based upon neither the prescription nor the proscription of human biological reproduction. Using contemporary environmental activism as a springboard, I point both to the mobilization of the Child as the privileged icon of a world to come, and to the anti-natalist tendencies implicit within recent accounts of a more sustainable future. Ultimately, I argue, we should look to foster a form of mutational politics – one that can be oriented towards practices of xeno-hospitality.

Chapter 3 addresses the topic of XF technologies via an engagement with the feminist health movement of the 1970s. This section – the longest of the book – looks to the sometimes problematic activism of the second wave, not to hold it up as an aspirational model, but in order to identify some of the possibilities contained within its partially pursued trajectories. What, I ask, might the DIY technologies of seventies self-help have to teach us about bodily autonomy and reproductive sovereignty from an XF perspective? The conclusion extends this analysis to encompass contemporary practices of biohacking. In deliberately eschewing the politically tone-deaf imaginaries of some forms of transhumanism, and by bringing biohacking into conversation with both trans* health activism and discourses of reproductive justice, I hope to emphasize some of the more materialist dimensions of twenty-first-century approaches to emancipatory, self-directed bodily transformation.

Whilst reproduction, in an expanded sense, remains at the forefront of my articulation of xenofeminism, other related themes will inevitably arise over the course of the book – themes such as scalability, labour, intersectionality, nature, and repurposing. Let us begin, however, by asking a seemingly simple question: what *is* xenofeminism?

I

# What is Xenofeminism?

XF is a *technomaterialist, anti-naturalist, and gender abolitionist form of feminism*. In this chapter, I will offer a brief outline of each of these three terms, using Shulamith Firestone's contentious manifesto *The Dialectic of Sex* as a recurring reference point. First published in 1970, Firestone's text claims that humanity's 'accumulation of skills for controlling the environment'[1] – extending, crucially, to gendered embodiment and biological reproduction – is a means of realizing 'the conceivable in the actual'.[2] It therefore looks to technology (including, most famously, assistive reproductive technologies, but also forms of domestic automation and industrial cybernation) as a point of leverage in efforts to transform oppressive socio-biological conditions. Her work adopts an ambitious, constructive, and wide-ranging approach to conceiving of a more emancipatory future. In this, it has profoundly shaped the xenofeminist imaginary.

## Technomaterialism

Xenofeminism is an attempt to articulate a radical gender politics fit for an era of globality, complexity, and technology – one which thinks about technology as an activist tool, whilst attempting to confront a contemporary reality 'crosshatched with fibre-optic cables, radio and microwaves, oil and gas pipelines, aerial and shipping routes, and the unrelenting, simultaneous execution of millions of communication protocols with every passing millisecond'.[3] It seeks to foreground the more obviously material elements of (inter)action in contemporary mediated cultures, and draws upon recent engagements with the digital that foreground its brute physicality over its supposedly more ethereal qualities – that is, over 'the cultural perception that information and materiality are conceptually distinct and that information is in some sense more essential, more important, and more fundamental than materiality'.[4] In other words, XF seeks to anchor that which has been frequently mischaracterized as free-floating and disembodied within its infrastructural requirements and within the obstinate physicality of its users and producers (including those workers engaged in repetitive and poorly paid labour on electronics assembly lines around the world).

The project does not reject technology (or science, or rationalism – ideas often understood as patriarchal constructs), but positions it both as part of the warp and weft of our everyday lives and as one potential sphere of activist intervention. Laboria Cuboniks takes a critical interest in technologies that might seem mundane, such as domestic labour-saving devices, as well as higher-profile innovations capable of acting as vectors for new utopias – things like pharmaceuticals, additivist manufacturing, open source software, systems of cybersecurity, and post-industrial automation. Just as these phenomena may be turned towards furthering the control and domination of labouring bodies, so too might they represent sites of fertile possibility for the feminist left. Xenofeminism is interested in exploring and leveraging these affordances – it 'seeks to strategically deploy existing technologies to re-engineer the world'.[5] At the same time, however, it recognizes that technologies are not inherently beneficial – indeed, they are not even inherently neutral – but are in fact constrained and consti-tuted by social relations. This includes specific design histories, the existing (technical, political, cultural) infrastructures into which they emerge, and imbalances in terms of who can access them – a factor largely dependent upon the character of the specific technologies in question.

Qualifications of this kind are common to many technofeminist theories and approaches. Even the enthusiastic vision of cybernetic communism laid out in *The Dialectic of Sex* displays some awareness of the limits that social context might place upon a technology's transformational implications. For example, Firestone appears cognizant of the fact that not only is her utopian project attendant upon the development of suitably sophisticated technoscientific capacities, but that 'in the hands of our current society and under the direction of current scientists [. . .], any attempted use of technology to "free" anybody is suspect'.[6] Even her preferred tools for feminist interventions in

embodiment are carefully problematized: reproductive technology, including birth control, is
described as 'a double-edged sword [. . .] to envision it in the hands of the present powers is to
envision a nightmare'.[7] Although hardly famous
for the moderation of her arguments, it is clear
that Firestone is attuned to the fact that the uses
of both computational and biological technologies will be dependent upon the wider structures
in which they are embedded.

In her response to *The Dialectic of Sex*, Sarah
Franklin remarks that Firestone 'envisaged technology both as an agent of, and a means of salvation
from, social and environmental degradation,
whilst constantly reminding her readers that science and technology could not achieve these ends
in the absence of radical social change, including
a wholesale regendering of scientific knowledge'.[8]
In Firestone's analysis, technology is presented
as both a 'driver and a symptom, imbricated in a
wider process of historical unfolding';[9] technoscientific developments must therefore be seen as a
significant influence upon socio-political change.
However, this influence is by no means unidirectional. The relationship between technology
and social relations is complex, mutually shaping,

dynamic, and dependent upon continuous conversation. Shifts in one area will influence the evolution of the other, which in turn feedbacks into further developments, in an ongoing process of co-constitution. Technology is as social as society is technical.

Technologies, then, need to be conceptualized as social phenomena, and therefore as available for transformation through collective struggle (a fact of which Firestone herself is well aware, even as she uses technologies to imagine a radically alien future). Technological change is a 'process subject to struggles for control by different groups', the outcomes of which are profoundly shaped by 'the distribution of power and resources within society'.[10] As such, any emancipatory technofeminism must take the form of a concerted political intervention, sensitive to the fused character of the structures of oppression that make up our material worlds. It is in this spirit that xenofeminism seeks to balance an attentiveness to the differential impact technologies can have upon women, queers, and the gender non-conforming, with a critical openness to the (constrained but genuine) transformative potential of technologies. This extends to an interest in how we might design or appropriate devices, knowledges, and processes for gender-political ends.

## Anti-Naturalism

Xenofeminism's technomaterialism is complemented by its commitment to anti-naturalism. Indeed, the project's investment in and alignment with contemporary technological landscapes is, in part, an elaboration of precisely this commitment. Hence, Laboria Cuboniks declares that:

> Our lot is cast with technoscience, where nothing is so sacred that it cannot be reengineered and transformed so as to widen our aperture of freedom, extending to gender and the human. To say that nothing is sacred, that nothing is transcendent or protected from the will to know, to tinker, and to hack, is to say that nothing is supernatural. 'Nature' – understood here, as the unbounded arena of science – is all there is.[11]

In other words, science and technology enable a particular set of conscious interventions within the so-called 'natural' world. Such interventions have the potential to extend human freedom – for example, by furthering reproductive autonomy and allowing us to exert control (however contingent, contested, and constrained) over what happens to our own bodies. Nature is understood here not as an essentializing underpinning for embodiment or ecology, but as a technologized space of conflict that fundamentally shapes lived experiences.

The always precarious distinction between nature and culture has been definitively blown apart by changes within science and technology. Whilst the collapse of such categorical distinctions arguably detracts from the utility of social constructivism as an analytic tool – particularly when it comes to exposing the mutability of identities – it simultaneously works to open up that which might previously have been viewed as untouchable (the 'natural') as a site of intercession and agency. This refusal to frame nature as only and always the unyielding limit to emancipatory imaginaries is a key element of the xenofeminist project, and a further point of resonance with *The Dialectics of Sex*. 'Pregnancy', Firestone writes, 'is the temporary deformation of the body of the individual for the sake of the species.'[12] She notes that gestation and childbirth are painful, risky, and beset with difficulties for the bodies that perform them. As such, she views the development of new reproductive technologies – including, but not limited to, those facilitating ectogenesis – as an unprecedented opportunity for ending the oppression of the impregnatable.

This is the belief motivating Firestone's demand that people should be freed *'from the tyranny of reproduction by every means possible'*.[13] This is probably the position with which she is most closely associated, and it is certainly the one for which she is most frequently castigated. There are indeed troubling aspects to her treatment of this issue, not least her apparent insensitivity to the eugenicist uses to which reproductive technologies might be put (a fact made painfully apparent in the raced and classed histories of sterilization abuse and involuntary tubal ligations). As Franklin remarks, however, much of the hostility directed towards *The Dialectic of Sex* has been somewhat neglectful of the text itself. As such, it 'remains important to ask what the positioning of Firestone as a naïve technological determinist and the frequent chastisement of [. . .] her claim that new reproductive technologies could bring about women's liberation reveals about the evolution of feminist debate over reproduction and technology'.[14] With this in mind, I would like to turn to a different feminist perspective – one particularly inhospitable to Firestone's line of reasoning.

The ecofeminists Maria Mies and Vandana Shiva have argued that 'science's whole paradigm is characteristically patriarchal, anti-nature and colonial and aims to dispossess women of their generative capacity as it does the productive capacities of nature'.[15] This strategic mobilization of nature and the natural informs much of Mies' work in particular, and can result in her adoption of somewhat eccentric critical positions. At one point in the essay 'White Man's Dilemma', for example, Mies argues that 'From time immemorial, women have dealt with pregnancy and childbirth in a creative way. But this creative process, this natural power, was not totally controlled by them, rather to a certain extent it remained "wild".'[16] This 'wildness' – the fact that pregnancy is something that occurs within the body without conscious deliberation or mediation – is supposedly part of what makes the whole process so enchanting:

The woman does not have a blueprint in her head according to which she makes the child. She may have fantasies, wishes, but the child that forms in her body, in co-operation with nature, which she herself represents and is, is not determined by her will. Ultimately, neither the process nor the 'product' are at her disposal. I think it is precisely this unpredictability that constitutes the newness of each child and provides the fulfilment that is being sought.[17]

This natural process is, of course, in direct contrast to technologically assisted reproduction, in which bioengineers are viewed as constructing the child as if it were a machine, made from isolated component parts. In this version of the reproductive process, human beings are in possession of a far greater degree of direct agency and control; ergo, the process loses its magic and is no longer experienced as 'creative, productive and spontaneous'.[18]

Mies' take on this phenomenon is to adulate the threatened wilderness of the cis woman's bodily interior, claiming that it seems 'obvious that what is sought is exactly the opposite of what the myth of modernity has promised and sees as positive: the total control of nature and natural processes by science and technology, the "civilizing", that is, taming of all "wild" forces of nature for the benefit of man'.[19] Despite Mies having earlier argued against reproductive technology on the basis that it 'alienates both men and women from their bodies'[20] – which is presented as being a self-evidently Bad Thing – it would seem that what is being venerated here is the fact of being alienated from the reproductive process *by nature itself.* Reproductive technology offers a disenchanted alienation, achieved via devolving epistemic authority to medical experts, whilst nature offers a (for some reason vastly preferable) *enchanting* alienation, achieved via the subjection of the impregnated body to forces beyond its control. This, apparently, is the source of the fulfilment human beings are looking for – the magnification of uncertainty, unpredictability, and disenfranchisement.

The apparent suggestion that gestation and labour should be beyond one's control is particularly troubling, given the myriad health risks still associated with pregnancy and childbirth. In her investment in natural alienation, Mies comes perilously close to romanticizing physical endangerment. It is also worth stressing the (rather obvious) point that such a position downplays the extent to which impregnatable subjects appreciate agential control over their own bodies. Indeed, a relatively high degree of bodily sovereignty is arguably one of the things that people value most highly about developments in the medical management of contraception, conception, pregnancy, and birth – as well as one of the things that many are most concerned to protect when it comes to differentially distributed and continually threatened access to abortion. Mies' love letter to disempowerment seems to bear little relation to the way in which many people experience the vulnerabilities and anxieties attendant on biological reproduction.

Unwelcome suffering, whether due to natural bodily processes or complex and repressive sociotechnical systems, does not offer an appealing basis for feminist politics, and is clearly untenable as a platform for emancipation. However, whilst celebrating the former implies an attitude of acquiescence (a serenity in the face of things that supposedly cannot be changed), the latter lends itself more obviously to an anti-naturalist politics bent on 'untangling what ought to be from what is'.[21] In other words, positioning the body as a potential site for feminist technopolitical intervention is one possible tool in a refusal to inevitabilize suffering. I am not trying to make a case for the inherently or essentially liberatory powers of technoscience here.[22] Rather, I wish to indicate a structural orientation within the xenofeminist project towards radical (re)composition and away from foreclosure. The future is under construction.

XF is an anti-naturalist endeavour in the sense that it frames nature and the natural as a space for contestation – that is, as within the purview of politics. Any political project based upon nature as a pseudo-theological limit, a cartography of the untouchable, or a space of incontaminable purity risks lending huge conceptual resources to the conservative punishment of radical difference. As we put it in the xenofeminist manifesto,

> Nothing should be accepted as fixed, permanent, or 'given' – neither material conditions nor social forms. [. . .] Anyone who's been deemed 'unnatural' in the face of reigning biological norms, anyone who's experienced injustices wrought in the name

of natural order, will realize that the glorification of 'nature' has nothing to offer us – the queer and trans among us, the differently-abled, as well as those who have suffered discrimination due to pregnancy or duties connected to child-rearing.[23]

With these comments, we position ourselves as Haraway's disobedient daughters. We too find 'discourses of natural harmony, the nonalien, and purity unsalvageable for understanding our genealogy in the New World Order, Inc.', and agree that it 'will not help – intellectually, morally, or politically – to appeal to the natural and the pure'.[24]

But to declare ourselves anti-naturalist is not to disavow the measurable and/or spontaneously occurring phenomena that structure our world, generate observable effects, and shape the horizons of possibility. Xenofeminism does not deny that there is a biological stratum to embodied reality, for example – that certain bodies have different susceptibilities and capacities (most obviously, in the context of this discussion, the susceptibility or capacity to incubate a foetus). What is *does* dispute, however, is the idea that this stratum is immutable or fixed simply because it is biological. On the one hand, this involves acknowledging the role that social ideas play in understandings of embodiment (including insisting that many notions about gendered bodies are ideological). More radically, perhaps, it involves framing the terrain of biology as itself rightfully subject to change. XF stands with those contemporary feminists who insist that 'biology is not a synonym for determinism and sociality is not a synonym for transformation'.[25] The operations of these realms are nowhere near so predictable.

Elizabeth A. Wilson contends that 'anatomy enacts the kind of malleability, heterogeneity, friction and unpredictability that feminist theories can relish',[26] and argues that we should 'recapture biology for feminist theory'.[27] XF agrees, and (as we shall see throughout this book) pursues an interest in an anti-naturalist nature at the levels of both theory and practice. Rather than cede this territory to conservative or corporate interests – which have, for several decades, been angling for the enclosure of biomedically manipulable bodies[28] – we must reframe the evident (if partial) changeability of nature as a space for emancipatory politics. As Firestone puts it, 'every fact of nature that is understood can be used to alter it'.[29] Biology is not destiny, because *biology itself* can be technologically transformed, and *should* be transformed in the pursuit of reproductive justice and the progressive transformation of gender. XF emphasizes what it sees as the fundamental mutability of bodies, identities, and the various processes that help to shape them; it recognizes the often violently denied plurality of spontaneously occurring gender diversity (as in the myriad forms of intersexuality); and is invested in a proactive and emancipatory reworking of the gendered and sexual order.

## Gender Abolitionism

The final characteristic I wish to consider is xenofeminism's agitation for the abolition of the binary gender system, which is to some extent built upon our commitment to anti-naturalism. If nature is folded into the domain of politics, and both norms and bodies are conceived of as malleable, then that which we currently think of as gender is one obvious domain of emancipatory transformation. But why talk about *abolition* in this context? If gender is available to be remade into something better, why not seek to rehabilitate it? Such questions relate to the avowed status of XF as a transfeminism. How may we square arguments for gender abolition with advocacy for less restrictive access to technologies of transition, and how can a project invested in maximizing trans* rights and freedoms make effective use of Firestone's perspective, given her seemingly rigid focus on dimorphic gender and reproductive embodiment?

In the previous section, we discussed the body's position as a reworkable platform, and the affordances that come with approaching it from a perspective of ontological anti-naturalism. It is in this context that *The Dialectic of Sex* retains its potential xenofeminist utility, despite the relative invisibility of trans* people within its diagnosis of gendered oppression. As Nina Power notes, 'Firestone's approach to the question of sex is refreshingly blunt. Sex difference is real. Men and women exist, and possess asymmetrical physical capacities which have historically made existence for women extremely difficult and frequently unpleasant or even lethal.'[30] Firestone observes, however, that with the development of increasingly sophisticated means of birth control and artificial reproduction, technology has 'created real pre-conditions for overthrowing these oppressive "natural" conditions, along with their cultural reinforcements'.[31] For a condition to be described as natural at this historical juncture is no reason to assume that it cannot be changed.

But however refreshing or otherwise we might find the expression of biological materialism in Firestone's work, there is much that needs to be negotiated or qualified in terms of her understanding of 'woman', especially if we aim to incorporate elements of her perspective into twenty-first-century transfeminism. *The Dialectic of Sex* insists that the sex-class system is based upon biological disadvantages suffered by those capable of conceiving, gestating, and bearing a child. In Firestone's account, this group is called women – but given that this term is a woefully inadequate label for the group to which she is referring, we may not wish to follow her in this. The position that will better enable us to put Firestone's ideas to use is one that recognizes the existence of various embodied differences (and the manner in which such differences have been culturally exploited) whilst understanding that it is a 'social act to reduce these to the existence of an irreducible dichotomy [. . .] correlating with the functional differences between participants in biological reproduction (remembering that "participants in biological reproduction," even potential participants, are a subset of the set of all human beings and not identical with that set)'.[32]

It is notable that, whilst elements of Firestone's perspective on gender tend towards the problematically dimorphic as a consequence of this focus on sexual reproduction, her work also agitates for an eventual end to the binary gender system. Hence, she argues that

> just as the end goal of socialist revolution was not only the elimination of the economic class *privilege* but of the economic class *distinction* itself, so the end goal of feminist revolution must be [. . .] not just the elimination of male *privilege* but of the sex *distinction* itself: genital difference between human beings would no longer matter culturally.[33]

She moves from reproductive embodiment (firmly equated with two distinct sex-classes) as *the* source of oppression and foundational division of labour, to a vision of the eradication of this oppression by and through the dissolution of gender itself. According to this vision, technologically facilitated changes in material experiences of biological reproduction allow gendered ideologies to be overwritten; the categorization of people on the basis of a limited set of physical differences is overcome.

This current within *The Dialectic of Sex* has led certain theorists to view it as an example of trans-positive second-wave feminism. Susan Stryker, for example, uses the passage cited above to argue that feminisms from the 1970s 'were not uniformly hostile to transgender and transsexual people'.[34] For Stryker, Firestone's gender abolitionism – born out of ontological anti-naturalism – is part of a 'vision of transgender inclusion in progressive feminist movements for social change'.[35] However, just as second-wave feminism includes a wealth of (sometimes incompatible) perspectives, so too does contemporary transfeminism. Not all trans* activist positions accommodate such a virulent strain of Firestonian anti-naturalism. Indeed, many organizations explicitly dispute any suggestion that being trans* might be considered a choice – a disputation which can manifest itself as strategic naturalism.[36] Such perspectives see nature not as a protean platform, but as both a stable origin and an incontestable endpoint – a view that is obviously at odds with xenofeminist ideas.

Within positions founded upon a claim of being 'born this way', one finds supposedly in-built characteristics leveraged as a kind of transcendental guarantee: 'we are told to seek solace in unfreedom [. . .] as if offering an excuse with nature's blessing'.[37] Problematically, the current 'politics of trans liberation have staked their claims on a redemptive understanding of identity. Whether through a doctor or psychologist's diagnosis, or through personal self-affirmation in the form of a social utterance, we have come to believe that there is some internal truth to gender that we must divine.'[38] Such concessions are understandable given the perpetually embattled condition of queer and trans* communities. Indeed, inevitabilizing one's own existence is a pretty shrewd move when labouring to ensure one's basic survival. However, XF would question the long-term utility of positioning these approaches as the primary form of trans* politics, given that they mark a retreat from one of the most radical and emancipatory tendencies of transfeminism: its capacity to operate as 'an arduous assertion of freedom against an order that seemed immutable'.[39]

This is in no way to position trans* subjects as particularly at fault for reinforcing the gender binary; this is the hallmark of a reprehensible Trans Exclusionary Radical Feminism bent on attacking those already 'most hurt by gender'.[40] Nor is this an attempt to 'deny the lived experiences of many of our trans siblings who have had an experience of gender since a young age'.[41] Rather, it is a move to 'acknowledge that such an experience of gender was always already determined through the terms of power'.[42] In recognizing the necessity of what the Black Panthers called 'survival pending revolution' – and insisting always on securing and broadening access to the juridical, medical, and social technologies of transition for all those who want them – we must not lose sight of our aspirations for what the 'revolution' itself might involve. As such, queer anti-naturalist gender abolitionism must claim its place alongside certain species of strategic trans* naturalism as part of any effective and multi-pronged ecology of activisms. What form, then, would a xenofeminist gender abolitionism take?

The first thing to note is that the designation 'gender abolitionist' is somewhat misleading. There are two key reasons for this. First of all, the term does not explicitly encompass the full scope of Laboria Cuboniks' ambitions. It is not just gender that we seek to dismantle, but various other structures that come to act as a (frequently naturalized – and thus rigidified) basis of oppression. We believe that traits associated not just with gender, but also with race, class, able-bodiedness, and so on, are unevenly loaded with social stigma, and often contribute to cultures of inequality.[43] Whilst the current political value of mobilizing around these categories does need to be acknowledged, xenofeminism argues that (in the longer term) the full range of these traits should be stripped of their social significance, and therefore of their ability to act as vectors of discrimination. To quote the manifesto, gender abolitionism is 'shorthand for the ambition to construct a society where traits currently assembled under the rubric of gender no longer furnish a grid for the asymmetric operation of power'.[44] The struggle must continue until currently gendered and racialized characteristics are no more a basis of discrimination than the colour of one's eyes, or whether or not one has freckles, or whether or not one can roll one's tongue: that is, until they no longer operate as the basis of a claim to a socially legible identity. In short, then, XF's gender abolitionism seek to unpick any culturally weaponized markers of identity that harbour injustices.

Secondly, the phrase 'gender abolitionism' risks coming across as a demand for the paring back of gender – a demand that difference itself be abolished. This is not what we are advocating for at all. XF is not a call for gender austerity, but for gender post-scarcity! It does not seek 'the eradication of what are currently considered "gendered" traits from the human population' – not least because, under current conditions, 'such a project could only spell disaster – the notion of what is "gendered" sticks disproportionately to the feminine'.[45] If anything, it is the *restrictions* upon gendered identity that we want to see scrapped; the tenacious binary thinking that continues to funnel identities into male and female, feminine and masculine, despite the obvious paucity of this model. Far from producing a genderless world, then, this form of abolition through proliferation is suggestive of a *multiply* gendered world. Xenofeminism is gender abolitionist in

30

the sense that it rejects the validity of any social order anchored in identities as a basis of oppression, and in the sense that we embrace sexuate diversity beyond any binary.

Laboria Cuboniks advocates for the system of gender difference to be abolished via the proliferation of gender differences – 'Let a hundred sexes bloom!'[46] This must go beyond insisting on recognition for a wider range of identity categories – a move which, as with the numerous self-categorizing options available to us on Facebook, can generate a 'plural but static constellation',[47] in which gender continues to bear the weight of signifying something beyond itself (attitudes, capacities, affinities, consumer behaviours, and so on). The aim of this proliferation is not the beautiful blooming of a hundred dropdown menu options, but the stripping away of social ramifications associated with the heterosexual matrix. Like some of our cyberfeminist forerunners, XF stresses the need to 'render gender laughable and obsolete in its frigidity and instrumentality'.[48] The recognition of *innumerable* genders is therefore only a first step in the refusal to accept *any* gender as a basis of stable signification.

To adopt such a position is not to suggest that 'we remain blind to differences among peoples and cultures and colours and sexualities and identities – as if that were even possible. But it does mean that we interrupt the chain of causality that all these categories imply in their formulation.'[49] For xenofeminism, gender should be granted no extraordinary explanatory power. We must look for more nimble and inclusive vectors of solidarity. XF is, amongst other things, a technomaterialst, anti-naturalist, gender abolitionist form of feminism. In the material that follows, I will trace out how these and other key xenofeminist traits might manifest themselves in relation to an expanded understanding of reproduction.

2

# Xenofeminist Futurities

Xenofeminism is invested in constructing an alien future. To do so, however, requires confronting familiar images of the time ahead – images in which futurity is reduced to the replication of the same via the social reproduction of today's hegemonic values, or in which it is rendered impossible due to projected climate collapse. How can one propose a forward-looking gender politics that takes contemporary conditions seriously without falling into either of these traps – oppressive conservatism, on the one hand, and debilitating hopelessness, on the other? In his 2004 book *No Future: Queer Theory and the Death Drive*, Lee Edelman famously takes issue with the future as a heteronormative construct, anchoring his analysis in the figure of the Child. This chapter considers the framing of the future within contemporary environmental activism, with particular reference to its mobilization of this figure.

For Edelman, the contemporary world is characterized by a reproductive futurism in which the 'Child remains the perpetual horizon of every acknowledged politics, the fantasmatic beneficiary of every political intervention'.[1] As he puts it, we encounter the

disciplinary image of the Child [. . .] on every side as the lives, the speech, and the freedoms of adults face constant threat of legal curtailment out of deference to imaginary Children whose futures, as if they were permitted to have them except as they consist in the prospect of passing them on to Children of their own, are construed as endangered by the social disease as which queer sexualities register.[2]

The needs of adults – particularly non-reproductive adults – are constantly subordinated to those of Children as bearers of the idea of the future. Edelman's primary examples of this phenomenon are rampant cultural homophobia and so-called 'pro-life' activism.

He argues that when we think the future, which is largely the terrain of politics, we inevitably perpetuate a culture that is laudatory of the Child, and therefore supportive of ideologies of the family that are both hetero- and homonormative. Whilst heterosexual sex and the monogamous, dyadic relationship form are socially sanctioned via the 'alibi' of biological and social reproduction, the queer comes to represent the 'violent undoing of meaning, the loss of identity and coherence, the unnatural access to jouissance'.[3] It is the irredeemable Other. The only proportionate response to this state of affairs is, for Edelman, refusal – the refusal of politics, the refusal of the future, the refusal of the Child. Those beyond the sanctified confines of heteronormativity are to embrace the death drive and to become what reproductive futurism has already decided that they are – just a bunch of selfish queers.

Edelman's work is quite clearly a polemic, gleefully spooking the straights and denouncing the 'fascism of the baby's face'.[4] As such it is perversely seductive – not to mention seductive in its perversity – and compellingly, charmingly, spiteful. It also alerts those of us with an interest in political activism to some of the risks inherent in framing the future. How are ideas about the Child and the family mobilized within contemporary activisms? When and how is this mobilization problematic from a queer and feminist standpoint, and in what ways can we fight for a better, more emancipatory future without relying on reproductive futurism? That is, how can we advocate for xenofeminist futures without falling back on an exclusionary and counter-productive imaginary centred upon making the world a better place for 'our' children?

## Pro-Nat(ur)al Politics

Climate change activism is particularly entangled with the envisioning of a world to come, given that it is fighting for precisely those conditions needed to sustain an earthly future – the environmental necessities upon which human and non-human life depend. Within climate change activism, the image of the Child often operates as handy rhetorical shorthand for the future itself, but (predictably) does so at the cost of inadvertently promoting the values of reproductive futurism. Ecofeminist perspectives, for example, are capable of providing nuanced analyses of the conceptual fusion of gender, race, and nature, yet can at times rely upon limited conceptions of the family and the Child. We frequently find women's role as environmental guardians attributed to their connection with practices such as familial care, subsistence farming, and social reproduction.

This is a solid approach, up to a point; understanding how material conditions and gendered expectations cultivate or restrict certain forms of knowledge can generate productive and important insights. However, the point at which a recognition of historical gender roles tips into an apparent naturalization of these roles is the point at which this approach loses its XF efficacy. It is a common criticism levelled at ecofeminism that it essentializes gender – that it links women with a biological capacity to give birth, and associates this capacity with a greater concern with ecology. Sometimes, these criticisms can themselves feel unduly reductive, dismissing a range of progressive and intersectional perspectives because of their emergence within a field with a reputation for gender essentialism. However, whilst important ideas have been developed within ecofeminism, it has at times failed to recognize how the discourse it facilitates might (perhaps inadvertently) mythologize femininity. Sometimes, this mythologization is fairly literal, as in Mies' 2015 essay 'Mother Earth'. This text discusses images of the Earth Mother as a recurring feature of pre-capitalist cultures, before the emergence of 'Man the Warrior',[5] thereby reinforcing a particular set of ideas about the gendering of care, violence, and so on.

This gendered mythology is accompanied by clear conceptualizations of the maternal role in environmental stewardship, with Mies claiming that 'Women, mothers, were among the first to recognise [environmental dangers], because they ask: What future will our children have in such a world?'[6] In speaking of women and mothers, Mies conflates these two social categories of personhood, implicitly advancing a biologized conception of womanhood as a reproductive role, and homogenizing what can count as 'women's experience'. To claim a central place for women within environmental struggles on the basis of assumptions about their biological and inherent social reproductive capacity, then, risks not only homogenizing but also essential-izing particular ways of doing gender. The risk of a project that accords women a special role owing to their embodied connection with mothering – a project that not only feminizes creation but also masculinizes destruction – is that the future terms of engagement around ideas such as other-directedness, responsibility, attentiveness, and so on, are restricted by their funnelling into existing gendered paradigms.

If womanhood = motherhood, and mother-hood = the ability to nurture, and all of this is grounded in a very particular image of dichoto-mized reproductive bodies, then there seems to be precious little opportunity for challenging (let alone abolishing!) hegemonic gender roles. Like all manifestations of nature, gender must not be confused with a pure and timeless structure – which is not to dismiss the centrality of gen-dered and reproductive embodiment within lived experiences or cultural constructions of the natural world. The challenge is to acknowledge the importance of, say, the gendered division of labour and the histories of familial forms without discounting the diversity of 'feminine' engagements with ecology or providing further discursive support for the idea of a binary gender system marked by inherently feminine or masculine practices and abilities. This is, of course, a very delicate balance to strike, but could perhaps be broadly characterized by a shift away from naturalized identities towards an appreciation of mutable, historically and geographically situated processes (of re/productive labour, for example) as a basis for xenofeminist solidarities.

Whilst Mies' work is a particularly clear example of the problems that can arise from conflating women, maternity, and a seemingly essential relationship to the environment, it's important to note that this critical position is not unique. In fact, it crops up with some frequency in contemporary ecofeminism. kaitlin butler and Carolyn Raffensperger, for example, suggest that women's 'roles as caretakers bring them close to natural cycles', causing them to see 'environmental threats to their children wherever they turn'.[7] Joy McConnell, meanwhile, argues that 'women's major role in civilizations around the world has been the bearing and nurturing of children and the welfare of families. Women have seen through our own experiences that everything is interconnected and interdependent.'[8] This supposedly generates a particular aptitude for ecological advocacy. At the very least, the way in which these ideas are articulated de-emphasizes the mutational possibilities within gender roles and familial relationships. Such positions are arguably in the service of reproductive futurism: that is to say, they assert the absolute centrality and importance of the Child for environmental activism as a result of their tendency towards maternity-centric accounts of women's relationships with proximal ecosystems.

## Somebody Think of the Children

Ecofeminist perspectives broadly align with mainstream environmentalism, which also makes frequent use of the figure of the Child. We might think here of the aesthetic framing of contemporary climate change activism in Europe and North America, including the imagery used to promote the 2014 People's Climate March in London, New York, Paris, and elsewhere. On posters spread across urban transit networks, one encountered an ethereal nymph-child, clutching a toy windmill whilst staring wide-eyed into the future. We could also include the UN's 2009

'Hopenhagen' advertising campaign, which was used to promote the Copenhagen Summit and to raise awareness about plans for a global climate change treaty. The campaign relied heavily on images of the young, and made particularly prominent use of white, blond-haired boys.[9]

The environmental advocacy project Environment Illinois, meanwhile, used an image of a small child riding a bicycle as part of materials to raise awareness about the health impacts of coal-burning power plants, accompanied by the slogan 'No Helmet Can Protect Your Child From Mercury Poisoning'. Writing about this image, Nicole Seymour points out that 'heterosexism in environmentalism often goes unnoticed and thus unchallenged, because it seems so sensible. To wit: the Environment Illinois ad expects an audience for whom the connection between reproductive futurity and environmental protection is a no-brainer.'[10] Its strategy also relies upon a mode of address that interpellates the viewer as a current or future participant in the process of species reproduction; we are hailed as parental protectors, in the expectation that we will unresistingly heed this call. Not only is the Child now a well-established cultural shorthand for a time to come (a time which is increasingly endangered by our actions in the present), but there is widespread social consensus that appeals on behalf of the Child must not be refused.

Indeed, as Edelman puts it, what value could be 'so unquestioned, because so obviously unquestionable, as that of the Child whose innocence solicits our defence'?[11] There are very few positions from which a call to act on the behalf of children can justifiably be resisted, and as such, this imagery can be thought of as an effective force of political mobilization. If the Child can be so utilized within the course of eco-activist struggles, then why protest against it? Surely, in the era of the Capitalocene, it's a case of 'whatever works'? The risk is that relying upon the rhetoric of reproductive futurity cultivates and fosters heterosexist discrimination – both in direct relation to ideas about protecting the environment, and more generally in terms of attitudes to gender and sexual dissidence. Indeed, the operations of reproductive futurism may foreclose the possibility of the 'xeno' by tying procreation to the endless propagation of the same – particularly in terms of structural oppressions, class values, and species chauvinism. As such, biological reproduction is rolled into social reproduction, in the sense that it is implicitly assumed to represent the generational transmission of inequalities.

The counterpoint of reproductive futurism within contemporary climate activism is fear of a queer planet. Discussing cultures surrounding public sex between men, for example, Andil Gosine writes that 'One of the most popular strategies engaged by police and other opponents of sexual activity in natural spaces has been to present themselves as protectors of children.'[12] Another 'commonly employed strategy towards this effect has been to equate sex with pollution, and to focus on the litter and damage to the environment produced by homosexual acts'.[13] In both of these approaches, queer subjects become pollutants, metaphorically and literally; a threat to both the social body (through their corrupting influence on children) and the so-called 'natural' world (through their excessive waste). Condom wrappers and lubricant are framed as environmentally damaging, and the response demanded is the eradication of public sex – rather than, say, the installation of rubbish bins in appropriate areas.

Not only does non-reproductive sexual activity

circulate as a kind of toxin within some forms of eco-activist discourse, but queer subjects are positioned as the *result* of the circulation of toxicants in others. As Giovanna di Chiro notes in her essay on the topic,

> the dominant anti-toxics discourse deployed in mainstream environmentalism adopts the potent rhetoric that toxic chemical pollution is responsible for the undermining or perversion of the 'natural': natural biologies/ecologies, natural bodies, natural reproductive processes. This contemporary environmental anxiety appeals to cultural fears of exposure to chemical and endocrine-disrupting toxins as troubling and destabilizing the normal/natural gendered body of humans and other animal species.[14]

There is a cultural fascination with animal indicators of toxic pollution that emphasize non-normative gendered attributes (abnormally tiny alligator penises, intersex rats with unexpected nipples) or sexual behaviours (co-habiting 'lesbian' herring gulls). The toxic effects of chemical contaminants, in other words, are positioned as manifesting themselves at the level of the compromised and polluted socio-sexual body.[15] These specific effects of contamination can come to be emphasized even above effects such as cancer – to be seen as more threatening, more disruptive. To quote one of the most influential popular texts on the topic – *Our Stolen Future* from 1996 – the 'danger we face is not simply death and disease. By disrupting hormones and development, these synthetic chemicals may be changing who we become. They may be altering our destinies.'[16] Mainstream anti-toxics discourse, then, takes a stand against a certain idea of the mutational in the name of an unaltered future.

The point here is not that eco-activism shouldn't concern itself with the effects of chemical contaminants upon gendered embodiment, or that to do so is inherently discriminatory; in fact, a number of transfeminist theorists have stressed the particular need for a proactive theory of synthetic androgens in an era in which hormones pervasively circulate as pollutants.[17] Alongside Michelle Murphy, I would argue that if 'living being is now hailed as alterable, and materially transformable in new ways, opening new possibilities for a malleable ontology of life, chemical injury calls for a more critical politics of alterability and greater attention to the kinds, modes, and exercise of power manifest in malleable life'.[18] Such attentiveness is crucial to any xenofeminist understanding of anti-naturalism and the technomaterial. It should nevertheless concern us that this environmental activism is 'hyper-focusing sexual anxiety around ambiguity, variability, and changeability',[19] with sexuate diversity being positioned as a kind of industrial accident.

As di Chiro notes, it seems unwarranted that popular science and journalistic coverage should choose to dedicate so many column inches to 'the seemingly unrelenting offensive on the stability and reliability of the human male reproductive capacity and sexual orientation'.[20] Alexis Shotwell agrees, pointing to the fact that many popular accounts of the dangers of toxicants choose to concentrate not on 'death, or pain, but rather a maldistribution of sex selection proportional to the norm'.[21] As she convincingly argues,

The subtext of this discourse is that feminization or queerness are harms to be avoided and reasons to pursue noncontaminated waters and bodies. The logic here is that straight and non-disabled bodily

formation – heterosexual practice and a hyposta-
tized cis/gender conforming body that lines up with
current classifications of who is disabled – are the
norm from which any form of difference deviates.[22]

An XF ecopolitics must combine an attentiveness to the biological strata of reality within
which bodies of various kinds can be affected by
chemical and other forms of potentially harmful
contaminants, with a rigorous anti-naturalizing
tendency and an unwavering commitment to
bodily autonomy.

There is a generalized over-reliance on ideas
about natural sexuality and gender within contemporary conceptualizations of toxic effects,
then – that is, there is a concern with reproduction as the means by which the future is secured,
not simply in terms of biomaterial conditions,
but in terms of normative socio-sexual conditions. The anxiety is not so much that the species
will cease to exist but that it might be mutated,
altered, or (xeno)feminized. What has been
stolen is the ability to guarantee sameness – the
unquestioned replication of established forms of
gendered embodiment and sexual subjectivity. In
this sense, of course, many of us might aspire to a

state of toxic queerness, labouring to undermine things-as-they-are in favour of different and more emancipatory futures. Here, in a different form, we encounter the influence of reproductive futurism as it trenches upon environmentalism: not simply a call for action on behalf of the Child, but the stigmatization of non-reproductive sex and improperly reproductive bodies.

## No Future for You

In positioning eco-activism as agitating on behalf of generations to come, we may unwittingly participate in the cult of the Child, which is so central in determining which lives are prioritized, whose needs are seen to matter, and which bodies are framed as threatening pollutants or undesirable side-effects of pollution. What does this mean, then? Should we throw our lot in with Edelman and his strategy of refusal? Should we join him in withdrawing from politics, dismissing it in its entirety as the terrain of family values? I don't think so.

Living for the now and saying 'fuck the future' hardly seems like an apt response to impending ecological disaster – and, indeed, the fact that

Edelman's analysis largely proceeds via queer readings of classic Hollywood films suggests that such crises are not really within his purview. *No Future* is not wrestling with the brute reality of the Capitalocene, so perhaps it is unfair to frame its arguments in these terms; and yet the undesirable implications of the text remain. For one thing, the mantra of 'no future' too easily parallels the neoliberal dogma that there is no alternative. Edelman's conflation of politics-with-the-future-with-the-Child does not hold in every situation: Nina Power notes that 'the question of a "queer" (that is, non-futural) resistance to communal relations has in fact been an issue for various twentieth century political movements. There have been various kinds of "queer" resistance to the organising principle of heteronormativity, which have at the same time been explicitly political projects.'[23] Power gives the example of the kibbutz movement – to which we might add numerous forms of eco-queer theory and activism.

I would also question Edelman's position from the point of view of solidarity with reproductive labourers. Whatever his position on actual caregivers, it is clear that he has precious little sympathy with the cultural figure of the Parent. Take this footnote from his introduction:

> 'Narcissism!' the cry will go up. 'Who, after all, [is] more self-denying, more willing to sacrifice, than a parent? Who more committed to hours of work without getting paid?' Not paid? Consult the ledger book of social approbation. Tax codes, baby registries, the various forms of parental leave: these, of course, all pale before the costs of raising a child. But pro-natalism's payoff isn't primarily measured in dollars or sense. It's registered in the universal confirmation of one's standing as an adult and in the accrual of social capital that allows one a stake in the only futures market that ever really counts . . . . [24]

The resentment is palpable here, even in the author's faintly begrudging list of the marginal financial supports associated with parenthood. Raising a child may well, for some, bring with it an influx of social capital to offset financial losses, as is plainly evident to those who resist the call of reproductive futurity and are refused access to that social capital. But one cannot live by social capital alone, and the exhaustion, impoverishment, and exploitation by white patriarchal capitalism of many caregivers deserves more than the dismissive treatment meted out here.

Of course, the vaunting of reproduction and the distribution of social capital are in no way evenly distributed phenomena. The wealthy, white 'yummy mummy' might be applauded for her contribution to the future of the nation state, but teenage mothers, black and Latinx parents, trans* and genderqueer subjects, immigrants, refugees, and benefits claimants receive no such treatment. This is painfully apparent in the history of medical abuse in the US, for example, in which black, Native American, Puerto Rican, and Mexican-origin migrant people experienced sterilization abuse in disproportionately high numbers.[25] The same unevenness holds from the point of view of the child. José Esteban Muñoz notes that 'In the same way all queers are not the stealth-universal-white-gay-man [. . .], all children are not the privileged white babies to whom contemporary society caters. [. . .] The future is only the stuff of some kids. Racialized kids, queer kids, are not the sovereign princes of futurity.'[26] All of this is very useful in that it prompts us to approach the givers and receivers of care in a differentiated way. It demands that we ask new questions: How can we support those engaged in social reproduction who do not enjoy even the relatively immaterial safety net of social capital? How can we act in solidarity with those who are depended upon by others and who make a huge (and frequently under-recognized) social and political contribution via their reproductive labour?

Muñoz's call for utopia is an important rejoinder to Edelman, and is instructive in the framework that it offers for thinking 'queer' – not contra the future, but as the unrealized, the emergent, and the still to come. He declares that 'Straight time tells us that there is no future but the here and now of our everyday life. The only future promised is that of reproductive majoritarian heterosexuality, the spectacle of the state refurbishing its ranks through overt and subsidized acts of reproduction.'[27] Rather than using this as a basis upon which to reject the future, however, Muñoz incorporates it into a rallying call for new and better futures:

It is important not to hand over futurity to normative white reproductive futurity. That dominant mode of futurity is indeed 'winning,' but that is all the more reason to call on a utopian political imagination that will enable us to glimpse another time and place: a 'not-yet' where queer youths of colour actually get to grow up.[28]

But whilst we can accept that utopia has a function in galvanizing the political imaginary, there are still insights from Edelman that we need to adopt and incorporate. Part of this involves being explicit about how our discussion of reproductive futurism intersects with ecopolitics and ideas about the Capitalocene. In acting on behalf of future generations, we must be careful not to foster 'the supreme value of species survival as a discursive technology of compulsory heterosexuality'.[29] As I have suggested, to the extent that we frame our activism as protecting the earth for 'our' children, we risk promoting restrictive, exclusionary, and xeno-inhospitable notions of whose existence counts.

Most obviously, by indirectly privileging lines of genetic descent and cultural inheritance, such approaches are distinctly speciesist; neglectful of the many other forms of life upon which environmental shifts might impact. How, then, can we think reproduction – even just in the sense of ensuring the survival of others into the future – without also reproducing the worst of reproductive futurity? At this point, I would like to turn to the work of Donna Haraway, who has done so much over the years in terms of helping us to view our species within its wider biological and technomaterial context. In recent years, Haraway has offered us a new slogan for an era of climate crisis: 'Make kin not babies!'[30] This is a call to synthesize new solidarities rather than to privilege genetic family and biological reproduction in a resource-depleted world. It is, quite clearly, a slogan in two parts: perhaps the easiest-to-grasp directive is the suggestion that we, as a species, should reduce our birth rate.

## Biopolitical Border Control

Official UN population projections now suggest that the number of people inhabiting the planet will pass the 10 billion mark by the end of the century, contributing to significant problems in 'food availability and affordability'.[31] Studies suggest that this situation may be significantly exacerbated by environmental crisis, with climate change resulting in global crop yield losses of up to 30% by 2080.[32] There are fears that the carrying capacity of particular regions may be exceeded, as local environments approach the maximal population load that they can support. This would risk detrimental effects not just on human lives, but on other species as well – hence Haraway's suggested check on fertility. 'Over a couple hundred years from now,' she muses, 'maybe the human people of this planet can again be numbered two or three billion or so, while all along the way being part of increasing wellbeing for diverse human beings and other critters as means and not just ends.'[33] Whatever challenges a surge in human numbers might bring, however, population density is but one factor in the complicated issue of environmental strain.

Any framing of the issue that lets capitalism off the hook is obviously insufficient and myopic. Wasteful and unsustainable methods of production, combined with learned habits of commodity and resource consumption, play a primary role in eroding the conditions that (quite literally) make lives liveable. However, whilst I instinctively feel that the more productive move might be to start from the systemic effects of surplus value extraction, I can nevertheless recognize the broad logic behind Haraway's call to make kin not babies – at least as far as it extends to the privileged, disproportionately resource-demanding classes of the Global North (a point to which I shall return). How is this call suggestive from an XF perspective? To the extent to which it fore-grounds alternatives to reproductive futurity, the process of eschewing the deliberate extension of one's genetic line – that is, of pollarding one's family tree – is intended to help us rethink modes of intimacy, sociability, and solidarity beyond the nexus of the nuclear family.

This brings us to the second part of Haraway's proposed slogan for the Chthulucene – making kin. This is the productive moment hitched to her negation of the current order. She declares that 'If there is to be multispecies ecojustice, which can also embrace diverse human people, it is high time that feminists exercise leadership in imagination, theory, and action to unravel the ties of both genealogy and kin, and kin and species.'[34] In other words, current ecological con-ditions demand a feminism that practises 'better care of kinds-assemblages (not species one at a time)',[35] and which prompts us to rethink the existences and relationships that our politics tend to privilege. 'Kin' is the concept that Haraway mobilizes in an attempt to cultivate this – an 'assembling sort of word' that speaks of solidarity beyond reproductive futurism.[36] In calling for the making of kin, rather than the making of babies, she intends to speak of a less naturalized, less inward-looking, and less parochial form of both intra- and inter-species alliance (one that can be adopted and practised by parents and non-parents alike).

We desperately need to qualify this rallying call *not* to make babies, however. When Edelman discusses what it means to 'resist the appeal of futurity, to refuse the temptation to reproduce',[37] he appears to rather sidestep the fact that biological procreation is not always an expressly planned or deliberately sought for process. Even if the provision of abortion was secure and the procedure itself culturally de-stigmatized, it seems likely that many pregnancies not planned for in advance would still, for complex and sometimes personal reasons, be allowed to continue to term. And of course, who would want to step in to forcibly prevent people from having children? I can hardly imagine Haraway advocating for the imposition of fertility control upon the unwilling masses! And yet, she could perhaps go further in disentangling herself from this idea – and, more particularly, from coercive histories of population management, extending to racist practices of sterilization 'as a kind of biopolitical border control, culling unwanted future lives from citizenship'.[38]

Indeed, it is important to recognize how Haraway's claims for multi-species flourishing based upon diminished birth rates can be considered 'symptomatic of a broad re-formulation of the deadly racial logic of mid-century eugenics'.[39] I am not arguing that to de-prioritize the making of babies is necessarily eugenicist, or that population should be 'the third rail of left political discourse',[40] but I *am* stressing the need to overtly and carefully navigate the histories of colonialist violence that this discussion brings in its wake. After all, even 'if universal flourishing is easier to imagine when fewer humans are in the picture, desiring fewer humans is a terrible starting-point for any politics that hopes to include, let alone centre, those of us for whom making babies has often represented a real form of resistance'.[41] As Angela Davis remarks, we would do well to distinguish between the 'individual right to *birth control* as a potential facet of reproductive sovereignty, and 'the racist strategy of *population control*',[42] which has historically marked a profound absence of such sovereignty.

Haraway does little to explain how her vision of population control might be made possible without violating individual bodily autonomy; her call for a reduction in human numbers seems curiously weightless, floating free of the entanglements and troubles with which she usually so doggedly stays. In one of her more recent texts, much-needed clarifications are added – she notes that 'kin making and rebalancing human numbers', for example, has to 'happen in risky embodied connections to places, corridors, histories, and ongoing decolonial and postcolonial struggles, and not in the abstract and not by external fiat'.[43] Indeed, she points to previous 'failed models of population control' as 'strong cautionary tales'.[44] And yet she still concentrates on a vision of reproductive futures in which human births globally are below replacement levels – a position that seems to begin from an assumed point beyond the capitalist present, rather than centring active struggles for a post-capitalist future. This makes the second part of the slogan, 'make kin not babies', a rather cumbersome critical weapon to wield.

When thinking about *biological* reproduction, we must not neglect the global operations of *social* reproduction that have such a profound influence upon the experiences of caregivers under capitalism. Rather than advocating for the reduction of human population size, it might be more appropriate to start from a commitment to acting in solidarity with the impregnatable and reproductive labourers. This is especially crucial in the case of those whose access to the social capital of parenthood is drastically limited – the world's displaced, racialized, impoverished, queer, and otherwise stigmatized subjects. It is crucial, too, that our futures engage with actually existing children (as opposed to the culturally inflated image of the Child that is typically mobilized in debates about the future).

This is not, to my mind, because of any special status to be awarded to the very young, but simply one expression of a generalized investment in, as far as possible, reconstituting refuge for the precarious and the oppressed. There is reason to hope, perhaps, that a reorientation away from reproductive futurity and towards various models of kinship and xeno-solidarity might actually encourage a deeper hospitality towards the Other, and that a generalized cultural rejection of the absolute privilege of the family line might be framed less as the dismissal of parents and guardians, and more as an act of solidarity with new arrivals of all kinds (from migrants, to new caregivers, to the very young).

## Xenofeminist Kin

With this in mind, I would argue that Haraway's demand to 'make kin not babies' can have utility only under specific and circumscribed conditions. It must be consciously and carefully positioned as a call for the fostering of a long-term ideological shift – that is, for an ambitious attempt to wrest hegemony away from reproductive futurism, and to open up alternative images of the future founded not solely on the Child. In this sense, 'A Cyborg Manifesto' was an early expression of the call to make kin. As María Puig de la Bellacasa reminds us, 'to avoid models of solidarity and resistance to domination that would expect us to rely on evident or given bonding and open ourselves to unexpected "unnatural" alliances'.[45] This is a position very much shared by Laboria Cuboniks.

The ground for our most productive strategic coalitions may not travel in our DNA, as trans-feminist movements have long been aware. Such movements have demonstrated the affordances of xeno-solidarity in the sustained and practical care they (have been obligated to) offer disen-franchised queer youth, estranged from the only solidarity network afforded substantial cultural visibility within the Global North – the family. Kin making, over and against baby making, makes sense when understood as a means of pri-oritizing the generation of new kinds of support networks, instead of the unthinking replication of the same. Such a move, expressly conceived of as a corrective to the lack of variety within (legally, culturally, politically) recognized and accessible ideas of kin, is important for a xenofeminist poli-tics. As we put it in the manifesto, 'the home as norm has been conflated with home as fact, as an un-remakeable given',[46] and we must make it newly possible to conceive of futures beyond the household, the family, and the Child as we know them.

This cannot take the form of a punitive disdain

regarding the reproductive choices of others (which would be against all the nuances of intersectional accounts of reproductive justice), nor can it take the form of a single-issue campaign for population control. Instead, it must be grounded in xeno-hospitality, in the opening up of currently curtailed choices, and in the creation of the ideological and material infrastructures required to synthesize new desires as accessible, feasible choices. This struggle is, of necessity, oriented towards post-capitalism, for 'we must engineer an economy that liberates reproductive labour [. . .], while building models of familiality free from the deadening grind of wage labour'.[47] Indeed, what I am describing here might be thought of as a form of counter-social reproduction – that is, as *social reproduction against the reproduction of the social as it stands*.

Encouragingly, Haraway approaches the end of *Staying with the Trouble* via a series of almost Firestonian images of alternative domestic arrangements. In a series of speculative, science-fictional vignettes about one possible future, she narrates a world in which conventional heterosexual reproduction has been replaced by post-gender, multi-parent genetic engineering.

In this world, 'Kin relations can be formed at any time of life, and so parents and other sorts of relatives can be added or invented at significant points of transition.'[48] Such imaginaries suggest a potential process of making babies that is *also* a matter of making kin – of bearing children without bearing the Child or investing in the social reproduction of white, cishet, patriarchal values. Perhaps a new variation of Haraway's slogan is required here – one which recognizes that the affective bonds we assemble within and against capitalism can take various forms, and need not perpetuate the replication of the same. 'Xenofam ≥ biofam' – the idea that families hospitable to otherness and synthesized across differences match or exceed those built on genetic coincidence alone – heads in the right direction, so long as we add the explicit caveat that so-called 'blood relations' can *themselves* become xenofamilial through an ongoing orientation towards practical solidarity.

If such a formulation still appears unduly dismissive about the possibilities of some forms of parental care, we might be forced to reach for something like 'xenofam > synofam', a formulation correctively favouring outward-looking solidarity with the alien, the foreign, and the figure of the stranger, over restrictive solidarity with the familiar, the similar, and the figure of the compatriot. We must, in a sense, defamiliarize the biological family, whilst refamiliarizing alternative networks of solidarity and intimacy in such a way that they can become both generalizable and maximally accessible, without falling into the trap of reproducing the same. Indeed, it is worth noting that reproductive futurism diligently neglects the alternatives to replication embedded within its procreative imaginary. As Rebekah Sheldon remarks, 'it is not just the case that the child retro-reproductively forecloses the future but also that the figuration of the child as the self-similar issue of the present, the safe space of human prosperity and a return to a manageable nature, forecloses the mutational in the reproductive'.[49] It is, in part, within the mutational that the xeno resides – in the perpetual possibility that repetition might enable the emergence of difference.

The monumental effort that goes into the avoidance of such 'transcription errors'[50] – as expressed in the reproductive futurism of mainstream environmentalism and beyond – reflects a pervasive cultural awareness that biological reproduction is, in fact, *separable* from social reproduction. Neither the genetic inheritances nor the carefully orchestrated upbringing of the embodied child can guarantee smooth generational continuity or exact duplicability. As such, a distinctive threat 'emanates from the notion, inherent in the idea of the future, that tomorrow may not resemble today, that is, that radical change is not only possible but also continuously operating within the logic of self-similarity and as the condition of reproducibility'.[51] Building upon and reorienting the work of Maria Mies, I would argue that it is here that the productive 'wildness' of reproduction must be located – not in the unpredictability of pregnancy and childbirth or in a refusal of the medical cyborg, but in the ever-present possibility of disruption against efforts to ensure replication of the same. Between one iteration and the next, a space is opened up whereby the alien may be admitted – hence, perhaps, the widespread aversion to and mistrust of real children (and their parents) that offsets any cultural fetishization of the Child.

Mutation is not a process that can be programmed in advance, but rather a phenomenon that might be encouraged, fostered, or facilitated via the practices of xeno-hospitality – just as the replication of the same is cultivated via the elaborate memeplex of reproductive futurity. Remember, kids: the future is fragile. What I have been proposing in this chapter is a broader dissemination of the material bases for means of survival beyond the nuclear family – for new formations of the socially reproductive unit that can enable the spread of a different system of values. This is a model for (re)producing futures without reproductive futurity, remembering that survival is the precondition for any revolutionary politics. I have argued that reproductive futurism should be considered a problem for those of us with an interest in eco-activisms – it is a trap that, as Edelman's work attests, risks tripping up anyone trying to think the future.

Much agitation on behalf of the Child – so often conflated with any world yet to come – tends to uphold heterosexist ideologies and monogamous nuclear family structures, as an inadvertent result of the discursive patterning that shapes our world. As Power and Muñoz suggest, however, there is more to the future than reproductive futurity. It is possible to have a politics beyond the horizon of the family, and it is possible to have a queer activism underpinned by the enabling affect of hope. Indeed, the judicious mobilization of such a future-oriented affect may be necessary if we wish to create conditions that are hospitable to re-engineering what is, for many human and non-human actors alike, an unbearable present. In the chapter that follows, I return to the theme of biological reproduction, not with an eye to abstract ambitions of population control, nor in celebration of the great white Child, but as part of an attempt to theorize what a xenofeminist technology might look like.

# 3

# Xenofeminist Technologies

The conversations we engage in on the future-oriented left 'too often revolve around the metaphysically inflated phantom of Technology as such rather than engaging the specific ways in which particular technologies are put to use for certain ends within distinct social assemblages'.[1] Against this tendency, this chapter will unpack the possibilities of a single technological arte-fact – the Del-Em menstrual extraction device devised by American feminists in the 1970s. I want to offer this device as a partial, imperfect, but hopeful example of what a xenofeminist technology might look like. Like the gynaeco-logical speculum, the Del-Em is a technology totemic of second-wave feminist self-help – a movement based around consciousness raising, self-education, and interventions in health and wellbeing.

Patented two years before the 1973 *Roe v. Wade* decision liberalized abortion legislation across the US, the Del-Em is designed to suction the endometrial lining from a human uterus, using a syringe and a flexible tube inserted into the cervix. This process takes minutes to complete, and was explained by feminists at the time as a means of regulating menstruation (by condensing the monthly bleed): 'rather than menstruating and cramping for five to seven days, a woman could have her period removed all at once'.[2] Professional physicians 'expressed concerns about lay practitioners using the device',[3] but activists saw menstrual extraction as a means of avoiding painful and prolonged cramping, as offering convenience and control, and as a tool in countering a generalized culture of shame around the reproductive body and its fluids.

Crucially, the Del-Em has uses beyond gaining control of one's menstrual cycle. It is also a means of preventing the establishment of early-term pregnancies, up to seven weeks after a person's last monthly period. As such, it is perhaps best known as a DIY abortion technology. In what follows, I want to briefly discuss the development of this device, and to explicitly frame it (and the social relations surrounding it) as a xenofeminist provocation. First, however, I would like to provide some broad context to the framing of reproductive technologies I will offer here.

## Specula(tions):
## Feminism, Technology, Trouble

The feminist health initiatives of the 1970s brought together what we might now understand as an ecofeminist scepticism about the capitalist (mis)use of technoscience with a qualified and provisional openness to technologies as gender-political tools. Although much feminist health activism sought to challenge the rise of technologized reproductive medicine, technology in and of itself was not subject to a blanket rejection. Instead, much of the effort to seize collective control from vested industrial interests was built upon the idea of appropriating established medical tools (the devices of insemination, abortion, and gynaecological examination, for example). As Barbara Ehrenreich and Deirdre English noted in 1973, self-help is 'an attempt to seize the *technology* without buying the ideology'[4] – that is, to disentangle potentially helpful devices from the contexts in which they are developed and through which they circulate.

Many of the technologies that were most visibly seized by second-wave feminists required little in the way of formalized expertise from their users. The gynaecological speculum (deployed in vaginal self-exams, in which participants looked at their genitalia with the help of a hand mirror) is perhaps the most prominent example. Given the simplicity of this device, it may not be particularly visible to us *as* a technology, especially when considered alongside the cutting-edge biotechnological developments of the time. Haraway, for example, states that this 'handcraft tool is inadequate to express our needed body politics in the negotiation of reality in the practices of cyborg reproduction',[5] and indeed, we must not lose sight of the fact that technologies with which we may be personally unfamiliar nevertheless exert a profound shaping influence upon our technomaterial worlds. Unlike some feminists from the 1970s, XF does not dismiss complex tools as inherently irrecuperable, but agitates for entering into debates regarding their design, implementation, and alternative affordances.

Self-help alone cannot hope to be a sufficient response to conditions of contemporary technological sophistication. Yet, given that the speculum is a tool still regularly used during routine check-ups (and one which carries a particular, often unpleasant, affective charge for those on its receiving end), it represents an immediate and embodied way into theorizing the medicalized cyborg. We should embrace 'multiple icons that reflect the range of technologies the cyborg confronts on a daily basis',[6] rather than automatically excluding the speculum and other relatively simple devices from our understandings of technological significance. For Terri Kapsalis, the handcraft tool, as 'menially mechanical and prepostmodernist as it may be, is still an integral part of the pelvic theatre'.[7] To dismiss or de-emphasize such lo-fi technologies is to neglect the important ways in which they continue to shape our experiences of technomateriality.

The tendency to dismiss domesticated devices – be they older, more familiar tools, or objects specifically associated with the mundane 'feminine' – as unworthy of attention radically restricts the scope of our engagement with technologies, and encourages us to overlook any ongoing dilemmas they might pose. There remains important work to be done in 'discovering the origins and paths of development of "women's sphere" technologies that seem often to have been considered beneath notice'.[8] In many ways, this chapter seeks to act as a corrective to this tendency. To be clear, then, handcraft tools do not represent the full extent of XF's horizons; as the text progresses, we will be drifting towards more overtly cyborgian forms of bodily intervention. However, I have selected my case study for its very particular affordances. It not only allows us to consider how XF's abstract theoretical principles might operate within concrete historical circumstances, but also directs critical attention towards a too often neglected area of technology.

It is worth noting that Haraway's account of the speculum is not entirely dismissive of its potential as a tool for gender politics, particularly when she positions it within the context of second-wave self-help. As she notes,

The repossessed speculum, sign of the Women's Liberation Movement's attention to material instruments in science and technology, was understood to be a self-defining technology. Those collective sessions with the speculum and mirror were not only symbols, however. They were self-help and self-experimentation practices in a period in which abortion was still illegal and unsafe. The self-help groups developed techniques of menstrual extraction, i.e., early abortion, that could be practiced by women alone or with each other outside professional medical control.[9]

The speculum, then, is (at first glance) a relatively simple technology, allowing people from the US and elsewhere to perform vaginal self-exams and generate some sense of their bodily autonomy outside of profit-driven healthcare. Indeed, this device continues to hold a central place in cultural imaginaries of feminist empowerment-through-health up to this day.

The current branding for the Women's Health Specialists of California, for example, features a raised fist clutching a speculum, and similar imagery appears on the front cover of the 2010 anthology *Feminist Technology* – a look at how the design, marketing, and use of particular objects might render them more or less helpful as gender-political tools. This choice of cover image is intriguing, given that specula are only mentioned twice within *Feminist Technology* – once, very briefly, as part of a passing comparison, and a second time as part of a discussion of their *limits* as a feminist technology. As one essay in the volume remarks, cervical screening and other gynaecological interventions are sometimes 'not particularly comfortable, in part because of the construction of the steel or plastic speculum itself. A quick patent search reveals that the speculum has not changed in shape or style much since the one designed in 1892.'[10]

Concerningly, the collection has nothing to say about the processes via which said speculum came into being – namely, through experimentation upon enslaved Black women. Its inventor, J. Marion Sims – a nineteenth-century pioneer of American gynaecological surgery – kept these women as 'property in the back of his private hospital'.[11] The speculum was developed in the context of prolonged experimental abuse, in which dehumanized test subjects suffered through multiple invasive procedures and operations without consent or anaesthesia. Specula, then, introduce some crucial caveats into the discussion of xenofeminism's penchant for appropriating technologies: such gestures *must* be attentive to the intersectional histories and entanglements of the tools they discuss. Otherwise, we might find ourselves in the position of uncritically celebrating the tools and products of torture.

## Removing Barriers

Aside from the speculum, the technology perhaps most closely associated with the feminist health movement is the Del-Em – a less widely recognizable, but nevertheless culturally significant, device for self-help. The Del-Em will be discussed here not as an isolated device, but as one key node in a network of interconnecting elements, including activist communities, healthcare infrastructure, developments in legislation, and transnational practices of care. For me, the Del-Em is an intriguing proposition for xenofeminist approaches to technology not simply because of its affordances for a limited conception of increased reproductive autonomy for the impregnatable, but for four other key reasons: (1) its circumnavigation of gatekeepers; (2) its status as a tool of repurposing; (3) its immersion in discourses of scalability; and (4) its potential for intersectional application. In what remains of this chapter, I'll address each of these points in turn.

The American second-wave self-help movement explicitly framed its activities as a means of restoring bodily autonomy to people who felt disenfranchised by their interactions with the medical establishment, and who were excluded from active decision making regarding their own care. As Ehrenreich and English put it, 'When we demand control over our own bodies, we are making that demand above all to the medical system. It is the keeper of the keys.'[12] The relationship between the providers and recipients of professionalized medical care in the 1970s was both highly gendered and deeply unequal, with service users 'dependent on the medical system for the most basic control over their own reproductivity'.[13] This was in the face of the threat of involuntary tubal ligations, unnecessary hysterectomies, and under-tested or unethically tested contraceptives.

Initially developing out of the consciousness-raising activities of the second wave, 'feminist self-help involved women meeting in small groups, sharing information and stories, educating themselves about their bodies and the medical establishment, and looking for remedies to minor bodily problems'.[14] Its focus was on developing lay knowledge not only as a means to assert immediate agency over one's own body – to more fully understand its workings – but also as part of a shareable process of self-enfranchisement and a first step in agitating for more patient-focused practices of care. Arguably, however, it is the movement's attempts to wrest control away from the medical establishment for which it is most famous. This DIY approach spawned initiatives such as the seminal women's heath book *Our Bodies, Ourselves* (*OBOS*) – first published in 1971 as the proceedings of a small self-help workshop that later became the Boston Women's Health Book Collective.

The collective faced many barriers to finding information about gynaecology and the reproductive body; it was often difficult for lay people to even get into medical libraries, and the writing process 'involved the clandestine borrowing of library cards from bona fide medical students'.[15] Much of the material included in the original edition of *OBOS* was the result of painstaking individual research in the face of scant information and resources – the sidestepping of medical gatekeepers and university librarians alike! Given the difficulties in obtaining even the most basic information about human health, the barriers in providing and accessing care beyond the professionalized medical establishment were remarkable. This was particularly the case when it came to procedures widely restricted by legislation. It was radical enough to include a chapter on abortion in *OBOS* (considering its publication two years before *Roe v. Wade*), but the need to widen actual access to abortion in the early seventies was particularly pressing.

The feminist response to this was to set up abortion counselling and referral services, such as Jane in Chicago. Originally established as one of a number of networks in the US intended to connect people with so-called 'backstreet abortionists', the group's activities later took a quite distinctive turn:

At first the women in Jane concentrated on screening abortionists, attempting to determine which ones were competent and reliable. But they quickly realized that as long as women were dependent on illegal practitioners, they would be virtually helpless. Jane determined to take control of the abortion process so that women who turned to Jane could have control as well. Eventually, the group found a doctor who was willing to work closely with them. When they discovered that he was not, as he claimed to be, a physician, the women in Jane took a bold step: 'If he can do it, then we can do it, too.' Soon Jane members learned from him the technical skills necessary to perform abortions.[16]

Through witnessing and assisting with the performance of abortions beyond a professionalized clinical environment, members of Jane developed a new understanding of and attitude towards the procedure: 'The techniques were very straightforward. [. . .] They were skills that, with practice and care', any lay person could learn.[17] With abortion thus demythologized, members of the service came to the conclusion that 'the barriers that the medical establishment erected between patient and practitioner were not a function of either a woman's needs or the needs of the situation'.[18] Instead, they were a function of disciplinary power and a means of hoarding both institutional authority and useful knowledge.

The group set itself a mission to further feminist reproductive sovereignty by making service users active participants in their own care – a process intended to denaturalize the condescending treatment that many received at the hands of doctors. Initially and primarily, Jane relied upon dilation and curettage abortions – a procedure in which the cervix is opened and the contents of the uterus are scraped out. Later, however, some members switched to a manual aspiration model using cannulas and syringes, which they learned about via the inventors of the Del-Em. Whilst Jane used methods *related* to menstrual extraction, rather than deploying the Del-Em itself, the accounts of those involved with the service remain useful to us for their critical engagement with medical instruments. Laura Kaplan organizes much of her history of Jane around the necessity of gaining 'access to the tools and skills to affect the conditions' of technomaterial existence – that is, she frames the circumnavigation of gatekeepers as a process of seizing technologies.[19] Again, we see that the development and appropriation of technology was a crucial part of the feminist movement's efforts to challenge medical sexism and profiteering.

The Del-Em itself, as a technology designed by feminists to route around the juridical and medical restrictions upon access to abortion, demands to be seen in just these terms. In this case, there is another level to the general tendency towards free information exchange and the bypassing of gatekeepers. The Del-Em arguably represents an engagement with the principles of free and open source design as a means of ensuring the equitable dissemination of tools and technologies. Whilst the device *was* patented by its original designer (Lorraine Rothman), it was always intended to circulate in a free and non-commoditized fashion. The formal turn to intellectual property was not about securing individualized ownership of menstrual extraction and its instruments, but was in fact a concerted attempt to ensure that the Del-Em would remain freely available, protected, and shareable amongst those who might need it.

This is important when contextualizing the emergence of the device, which was designed in California during the 1970s – a time and space associated with considerable innovation in software development. The emphasis on shareability associated with self-help in general, and with menstrual extraction in particular, can be thought of as 'analogous to modes of shared and circulated production that gave birth to software such as UNIX, and later LINUX, as well as the open-source patent'[20] – developments which some contemporary commentators see as suggestive of the rise of a new economy of contribution, grounded upon participatory knowledge exchange. An emerging interest in free and open source design and dissemination was characteristic of the Del-Em's historical moment. In its commitment to non-market mechanisms, and its focus on information sharing and voluntary cooperation, the feminist self-help movement arguably demonstrates an ethos akin to that of what we now call the Creative Commons; this was one key prong of feminist efforts to work around oppressive pathways of healthcare.

The xenofeminist manifesto touches upon the link between medical technologies and free and open source platforms in a different context – namely, healthcare for trans* people in the twenty-first century. Paul B. Preciado is amongst those who have discussed the bypassing of gatekeepers within trans* communities. His ground-breaking book *Testo Junkie: Sex, Drugs, and Biopolitics in the Pharmacopornographic Era* describes his self-experimentation with Testogel – a synthetic androgen administered through the skin. As he remarks, whilst some people choose to use the drug 'as part of a protocol to change sex', others are 'self-medicating without trying to change their gender legally or going through any psychiatric follow-up'.[21] Preciado positions himself within this latter camp, taking testosterone outside of the narrowly defined territories of its institutionally sanctioned usage. He is not taking it with the permission of doctors in order to transition from 'female' to 'male'; he is illicitly self-administering it, appropriating and repurposing specific molecules in an act of auto-experimentation without preconceived goals or ideal outcomes.

The decision to not seek an official diagnosis is in part a refusal to submit to the policing gaze of medical and juridical authorities. As Joshua Rivas observes in his engagement with *Testo Junkie*:

Before a transgender individual can generally be prescribed a course of hormone replacement therapy (and in France have its associated costs covered by social security), the trans-person must first meet certain minimum eligibility criteria set forth in the

Harry Benjamin International Gender Dysphoria Association's *Standards of Care*, including diagnosis with a gender identity disorder by a mental health professional or physician. Preciado in this way situates herself [*sic*] within a biopolitically constructed space of clandestinity and non-recognition . . . .[22]

Some commentators see this dynamic as characteristic of wider tensions between trans* communities and disciplinary powers in the Global North, arguing that trans* people 'seek access to surgical, hormonal and psychotherapeutic treatments, but seek to avoid pathologisation and stigmatisation – this is a defining characteristic, perhaps the central dilemma, of their relationship with clinicians'.[23] This dilemma is one reason why some people with the means to do so might choose to sidestep an official diagnosis as a means of accessing treatments and technologies. As with feminist self-help in the 1970s, a fractious relationship with healthcare infrastructures drives people to find different ways of accessing care, often tied to self-experimentation within politicized support networks.

The grasp of gatekeepers upon both knowledges and technologies has loosened significantly in recent years, however, as reflected by clinical guidelines. The Royal College of Psychiatrists notes that 'Hormones and hormone-blockers are readily available via the internet. The medical practitioner or specialist must consider the risks of harm to the patient by not prescribing hormones in these circumstances.'[24] The guidance, therefore, is that GPs or other non-specialist medical practitioners 'prescribe "bridging" endocrine treatments as part of a holding and harm reduction strategy while the patient awaits specialised endocrinology or other gender identity treatment'.[25] We can see that having alternative means of accessing information, peer support, and pharmaceuticals has forced profound changes in the way the medical establishment conceives of treatment. This represents a new means of resisting those institutions that have historically fought to restabilize the disciplinary grid of gender in the face of biotechnical innovations that might unsettle it.

By taking testosterone in an unsanctioned fashion, Preciado uses technical intervention within and upon the body as a means of contesting the pharmacopornographic regime that constitutes him. He expresses this quite forcefully at times, insisting that 'your body, the body of the multitude and the pharmaco-pornographic networks that constitute them are political laboratories, both effects of the process of subjection and control and potential spaces for political agency and critical resistance to normalization'.[26] In a move that clearly resonates with self-help's privileging of the lay healer, Preciado explicitly frames auto-experimental engagements with embodiment as part of a tradition of radical amateurism. This is associated particularly with herbalists, midwives, and witches – practitioners who were deliberately excluded from medicine in order to enable its simultaneous professionalization and masculinization. Preciado claims that the coming of modernity involved a widespread 'process of eradicating knowledge and lower-class power while simultaneously working to reinforce the hegemonic knowledge of the expert, something indispensable to the gradual insertion of capitalism on a global scale'.[27] Networked communication technologies, however, have made it increasingly difficult to continue stockpiling knowledge in exclusionary ways.

Interestingly for our purposes, Preciado frames his institutionally illegitimate relationship with

Testogel in language more generally associated with digitality and the Creative Commons. He throws in his lot with 'gender hackers' – a community of '*copyleft* users who consider sex hormones free and open biocodes, whose use shouldn't be regulated by the state or commandeered by pharmaceutical companies'.[28] The means by which biotechnologies and information can circulate in the digital age has, XF argues, been 'instrumental in wresting control of the hormonal economy away from "gatekeeping" institutions seeking to mitigate threats to established distributions of the sexual'.[29] This includes 'the hydra of black market pharmacies' that have been made accessible in the digital age, as well as the dissemination of 'endocrinological knowhow' amongst online communities – phenomena in part buoyed by increasingly visible developments in cryptocurrency and darknet marketplaces.[30]

The rise of the internet, in other words, has brought with it new opportunities for people to route around juridical and medical institutions, and thereby to refuse (to a certain extent) limiting and unhelpful forms of pathologization. However, the xenofeminist manifesto articulates a dissatisfaction with the limited alternatives provided by illicit online commerce – not least because of the potential for unregulated pharmacies to sell inefficacious counterfeit medication, drugs that have been improperly stored, and so on. In a further point of crossover with the ethos of the Creative Commons, we write that

> To trade in the rule of bureaucrats for the market is, however, not a victory in itself. These tides need to rise higher. We ask whether the idiom of 'gender hacking' is extensible into a long-range strategy, a strategy for wetware akin to what hacker culture has already done for software. [. . .] Without the foolhardy endangerment of lives, can we stitch together the embryonic promises held before us by pharmaceutical 3D printing ('Reactionware'), grassroots telemedical abortion clinics, gender hacktivist and DIY-HRT forums, and so on, to assemble a platform for free and open source medicine?[31]

In looking to these sites, we are acknowledging glimmering moments of opportunity within what is, in many ways, a restrictive and conservative online landscape. In pointing to these limited affordances, I would argue that we are also engaging with the legacy of the Del-Em.

It may seem perverse to contextualize contemporary trans* practices and activisms in terms of a second-wave feminist movement not known for its hospitability to anybody but cis women – and white, middle-class, First World, cis women at that. Even twenty-first-century accounts of seventies self-help typically fail to address its implicit exclusion of Othered bodies. It is rare that the important implications of the movement for trans*, non-binary, intersex, or gender-nonconforming people are considered, despite this being one of its most interesting legacies. How can our transfeminist practice negotiate these falsely universalizing tendencies? How can the Del-Em be an example of a xenofeminist technology, given the seeming invisibility of trans* (non-)reproductive bodies within the context from which it emerged?

This is an issue to which we will return later in the chapter. For now, however, we can simply note that XF is engaged in an uneasy entanglement with the self-help movement. For this entanglement to be productive, we will need enter into a process of active repurposing – a process one might characterize as using old means for new ends. All acts of repurposing represent a kind of reclaiming or redirection of past activities, and this chapter's specific use of examples drawn from second-wave feminism demands a reorientation of the movement towards new ends, a concerted extension of its goals, and a strategic appropriation of its tools.

## (Re)purposeful Activity

Bringing the second-wave feminist health movement and its 'handcraft tools' into conversation with more recent developments in digital culture may seem like a stretch. However, I am not the first author to identify self-help as a resource for thinking about networked communication in the twenty-first century. Alexandra Samuel, for example, looks to menstrual extraction not as a point of synergy with open source software, but as a model for alternative telecommunications networks during states of emergency. More specifically, she considers the importance of grassroots self-reliance in an era in which the internet (as a vital system of memory and know-how) has become an essential survival tool.

Samuel notes that, in times of crisis, 'our ability to reach emergency responders, access life-saving information, and track down our friends and family largely depend on our ability to place a call or connect to the Internet. In a disaster, that connectivity can be one of the first things to go.'[32] Being post-millennial cyborgs, our capacity to act is largely tethered to the everyday informational infrastructures with which we engage. As such, we may find ourselves in need of alternative communicational technologies in the event of a crisis – this includes everything from basic ham radios to decentralized networks assembled through interconnecting 'Internet of Things' devices. Indeed, such networks would be valuable not only in emergency situations in which communications infrastructure is brought down, but also in cases of state censorship, inequitable access to the internet, and other barriers to the free flow of information. We might consider the shutting down of peer-to-peer filesharing or whistleblowing sites here, as well as situations of civil uprising.[33]

Samuel remarks that 'we should radically expand the number of people who have the technical know-how, hardware, and emergency power to set up and sustain a peer-to-peer mesh network. [. . .] The hardware and power required

to keep a network node running are not monumental, and the tech know-how required, while
significant, is within reach of anyone who can
follow written instructions.'[34] The most urgent
requirement, as far as she is concerned, is an
appropriate bottom-up movement centred
on self-equipping via knowledge exchange – a
movement that teaches the widest possible range
of people how to bypass official channels, given
that maximum participation facilitates more
robust mesh networks. Whilst this focus on
defensiveness is arguably somewhat at odds with
tendencies in the xenofeminist manifesto (a point
to which we shall return in due course), Samuel's
discussion nevertheless chimes with our analysis by explicitly extending to the feminist health
movement of the 1970s.

Menstrual extraction is positioned here as a
model of, and a precedent for, 'a long-standing,
decentralized campaign that disseminated complex technical skills to a wide range of would-be
self-helpers'.[35] The argument brings the knowledge practices of self-help – including its assembly
and use of the Del-Em – into conversation
with the contemporary need to extend technical literacy regarding alternative communication

infrastructures: 'The example of menstrual extraction proves that it is possible to disseminate both the gear and expertise required for a moderately challenging form of self-help. What it takes is a small community of committed, knowledgeable people who are ready to teach, and a larger community of people who see the value in learning.'[36] Whilst Samuel's argument concentrates on the DIY element of this strand of American second-wave activism – its capacity to sidestep gatekeepers, discussed above – it also touches upon the second of my four trajectories for XF technologies. It is an example of *repurposing*. In the case of peer-to-peer mesh networks, it is mundane, 'battery-powered, Bluetooth-enabled gadgets' that are strategically appropriated.[37] By turning these devices towards purposes other than those for which they were primarily designed, a network can be created that, by linking to other local networks, forms a wider assemblage of connection.

This vision of a grassroots movement for technical literacy, then, is partially driven by ideas about reusing and repurposing accessible resources in as effective a way as possible. The Del-Em is certainly an example of that. Indeed, strategic appropriation of this kind is important to consider when discussing potential points of confluence between menstrual extraction and the xenofeminist project. In the manifesto, we question why there has been so 'little explicit, organized effort to repurpose technologies for progressive gender political ends', and advocate for the strategic redeployment of 'existing technologies to re-engineer the world'.[38] At this point, it may be worth noting that sociotechnical developments in general can be conceived of as a form of repurposing, in that they turn extant materials towards alternative uses; this is simply the flipside of the truism that every possible transformation emerges from existing conditions and is constrained by the materials at hand. However, there is a more specific point to be made here.

In a recent interview, my Laboria Cuboniks collaborator Lucca Fraser was asked whether she thought the master's tools could ever dismantle the master's house. Her response was emphatic:

Yes. Both literally and figuratively yes. That's what tools are – they've got uses that go beyond their masters' intentions. And they've got weaknesses that can be exploited to make them do things they weren't intended to do. Which is basically what hacking means. This doesn't mean we shouldn't invent new tools. The more the better. But yes, absolutely, the master's tools can dismantle the master's house.[39]

Not only can we draw upon existing resources to develop better tools, then, but we can also draw upon existing tools to pursue better, more emancipatory outcomes. These comments clearly chime with my characterization of repurposing as using old means for new ends, and resonate with much of my conception of menstrual extraction technologies. The Del-Em, in many ways, seeks to enact something like a xenofeminist project of repurposing, and gives concrete form to abstract discussions about disobedient tools.

The most obvious sense in which it achieves this is through the process of its material construction. Rather than being purchasable as a complete, ready-made object, the expectation was that auto-experimental self-help practitioners would build the device themselves, perhaps by repurposing everyday artefacts from their own homes – aquarium piping; a mason jar of 'the kind used for home canning'; the plastic tube from a can of hairspray; and so on.[40] As with mesh networks, we see that this pragmatic seizure of elements from the mundane technosocial world is closely connected to the project of circumventing gatekeepers.

For its designers, the Del-Em

> held the promise that women might learn to safely perform this procedure on each other, making it almost impossible for the state to enforce restrictive laws. It was important to Rothman and her allies that other women who had no prospect of medical abortion – such as in prisons – could build her device with parts found at grocery, hardware, and pet stores.[41]

Beyond this clever redeployment of workaday objects, however, the device as a whole can be thought of as repurposeful, given the history of its emergence. The Del-Em was inspired by the portable equipment used by a number of backstreet abortionists, with Rothman's patent adding only a valve, some tubing, and a collection jar to the existing design.[42] These illicit, twentieth-century practitioners needed efficient tools that were maximally safe to use outside of a clinical setting. The feminist self-help movement shared these needs, but sought to make the technology further accessible; it wanted to eradicate the trauma of having to seek out covert procedures, and to secure the device's status as non-commercial.

In the case of the Del-Em, a technology originally designed to make a profit from the suffering of the unwillingly pregnant was tweaked, patented, and used for explicitly feminist aims. Underground abortion in the US is by no means the starting point of the Del-Em's travels, however, and nor is it the first link in its chain of appropriations. The device is actually the result of (and a contribution to) an ongoing transnational history of reproductive politics, population control, and tussles around bodily sovereignty. An increased state interest in family planning in China before the Cultural Revolution is one key branch of the Del-Em's genealogy, for example. This was a period of intensified research into new methods of abortion, as techniques were envisioned that might prove efficient in rural areas of the country, including a negative pressure bottle method of aspiration that 'used a glass bottle heated with a match to create a vacuum, and hence did not require electricity to create suction'.[43] Given that this device was especially designed to circulate outside of clinical settings – and thus for use by people other than doctors – it was of particular interest to some American pro-choice feminists before *Roe v. Wade*.

According to Michelle Murphy,

> images of this technology clipped from a Chinese nursing journal article circulated among East Coast radical feminists in the late 1960s, repoliticized as a possible means of providing abortions without medical involvement [. . .] . Thus, the itinerary of the device begins not with a movement from the West to elsewhere, but from the so-called communist third world to a Western imperial centre.[44]

Such processes of transnational knowledge exchange were not uncommon within the feminist health movement. *OBOS*, for example, travelled widely after its initial publication, but rarely arrived at its destinations unchanged. The text's various translators – often local activist groups – 'invariably participated in a collective process of contextualizing and critically reworking the US text'.[45] Such reworkings often directly confronted difference, rather than skimming over potential conflicts, in order to 'open up contro-versial topics, celebrate local accomplishments, or suggest points for political coalitions'.[46]

As with technical knowledge about abor-tion, this process of selective appropriation and recontextualization was not simply a matter of ideas being disseminated from North America outwards: 'its flows were not unidirectional. The text not only moved from place to place, but its translations travelled as well, providing the basis for new translations or returning – literally – to the United States, where they were taken up and used by diasporic communities.'[47] Such processes led to the US edition of the text being revised, extended, and qualified in response to the per-spectives of those who saw fit to challenge it. This may in itself be considered a form of critical femi-nist repurposing. After all, we have seen that acts of strategic, technomaterial appropriation can take various forms – the utilization of intellectual property law to protect a technology's free circu-lation; the exploitation or reassembly of existing objects for unexpected purposes; the modification of reproductive technologies in order to extend bodily autonomy or foreground feminist values. So far in this chapter, I have used the Del-Em to explore and develop two key principles of XF: (1) the circumnavigation of gatekeepers; and (2) processes of repurposing. In the section that follows, I will consider what insights might be gleaned regarding scalability.

## The Scale of the Problem

Menstrual extraction took the individualized solution of illegal abortion, and reimagined it as a *political* solution, focused around communities of feminists carving out their own spaces of reproductive sovereignty. The role of this communal process was significant for the self-help movement – both as a physical necessity, given that 'it wasn't possible for a woman to insert the tubing by herself',[48] and as itself a form of feminist consciousness-raising technology. Indeed, this is arguably what sets the Del-Em apart from other, related efforts at fertility control in the 1970s. During this period, various procedures were coming into existence for manually evacuating the content of the uterus via vacuum aspiration – not just those of backstreet abortionists, but also those of more or less state-tolerated practitioners in countries like

Bangladesh. One thing that clearly differentiated the Del-Em from these other projects was the collectivized, politicized contexts in which it was deployed. This brings me to another element of this technology that resonates with xenofeminist interests: its scalability.

Self-help, menstrual extraction, and the Del-Em all demand to be seen as primarily local interventions. Whilst they have considerable implications for individual reproductive autonomy and shifts in subjectivity, there are obvious material limits to what self-help can achieve on its own. As Ehrenreich and English remarked at the time,

> It *could* expand far beyond self-examination to include lay (though not untrained) treatment for many common problems – lay prenatal and delivery assistance, lay abortions, and so on. But if our imaginations are unlimited, our resources *are* limited. If we are concerned with the care of *all* women – and not just those with the leisure for self-help enterprises – for *all* their problems – and not just the uncomplicated disorders of youth – then we are once again up against the medical system with its complex and expensive technology.[49]

Ultimately, a knowledge of one's own body and its processes can take one only so far. At a certain point, reliance upon wider healthcare infrastructure will resurface. After all, to 'secede from or disavow capitalist machinery will not make it disappear. Likewise, [. . .] the call to slow down and scale back is a possibility available only to the few.'⁵⁰ Such comments apply as much to self-help as they do to anarcho-localist visions of the commune. Withdrawal is largely possible only for the 'healthy' – with health understood as a differentially distributed privilege, generative of other privileges, the experience of which is inevitably shaped by structural oppressions or advantages.

An example from routine healthcare practices illustrates this point. Cervical screening is a regular experience for many people in high-income economies (although the distribution of both preventive screening and reactive care remains disturbingly uneven). The smear test was first introduced as a routine screening technique in the US in the 1940s. At this time, the inventor of the Pap smear raised the possibility of subjects self-collecting cells from their own cervixes, advising that to do so would not affect a sample's quality. However, 'the profession of gynaecology was reluctant to give authority over the smear to women themselves, instead absorbing the smear as a key practice within a reorientation of gynae-cology that [. . .] brought increasing numbers of women under its care'.[51] Given its relative sim-plicity and its ties to disciplinary power, then, the cervical smear test represents particularly fertile territory for feminist self-help.

Several second-wave collectives and feminist health centres did indeed take an interest in Pap smears – Jane, for example, extended its remit to include cervical screening in around 1971. Upon realizing that many of the people it was serving were reliant upon welfare or a minimum-wage income, the largely white and middle-class group decided to provide additional basic gynaecologi-cal services. The illegal abortionist its members were learning from donated a teaching micro-scope, and from that point onwards, Jane began offering all of its service users a free Pap smear.[52] Whilst this may seem like a clear example of self-help successfully enacting some of its own key tenets, there were limits to what could be achieved in this informal context.

Kaplan remarks that, although Jane mem-bers 'stained the slides [. . .] they didn't have the expertise to recognize differences in cell structure'.[53] This eventually led the network to partner with a professional laboratory; the 'total cost to the group for each Pap smear, including materials and lab charges, was under $4'.[54] Despite the low cost, however, the 'movement of the Pap smear from participatory clinic to lab drew the limits of feminist self-help's scale of action'.[55] The reliance upon conventional healthcare infrastructure, even in the case of a relatively simple procedure, indicates that totally autonomous medical care is nearly impossible to maintain in an era of increasingly complex biotechnological entanglement.

Despite these limits, however, the discourse surrounding the Del-Em still provides a productive (though partial) model for a xenofeminist politics of scale. That is to say, it offers practical guidance in terms of how 'a mobile and intricate network of transits' might be facilitated between the micro- and the macropolitical levels of emancipatory feminist politics.[56] This is because the development of the Del-Em as a technology was accompanied by the development of menstrual extraction as a collective process; concerted efforts were made to ensure that it could circulate beyond the atomized emptying uterus. Indeed,

Murphy argues that the activists involved in the dissemination of the Del-Em were engaged in 'a kind of *protocol feminism* – a form of feminism concerned with recrafting and distribution of technosocial practices by which the care and study of sexed living-being could be conducted'.[57] Such a formulation strikes me as rich and stimulating, but how are we to understand the concept of protocol in this context? What does feminism have to gain from being appended to it?

The work of Alexander Galloway and Eugene Thacker may offer some insight here. In *The Exploit*, they argue that the concept of protocol can be defined as 'a horizontal, distributed control apparatus that guides both the technical and political formation of computer networks, biological systems, and other media'.[58] The protocol, in other words, is understood as a decentralized means via which to guide the formation of various networks – an 'apparatus of organization' with implications far beyond conventional information technologies.[59] Indeed, I would argue that the protocol as a social or political technology has greater resonance with the current discussion than does the protocol in its merely technical sense (as in hypertext transfer protocols and so on).

Galloway and Thacker outline several key characteristics of protocol, but I wish to concentrate on the three I consider most immediately relevant for the articulation of protocol (xeno) feminism:

1    Protocols are *relational*. They 'emerge through the complex relationships between autonomous, interconnected agents'.[60]

2    Protocols are *adaptive*. In order to 'function smoothly, protocological networks must be robust and flexible; they must accommodate a high degree of contingency through interoperable and heterogeneous material interfaces'.[61]

3    Protocols are *organizational*. They can be understood as an 'emergent property of organization and control in networks that are radically horizontal and distributed'.[62] As such, they represent the exercise of influence upon decentralized networks.

The affordances of such a conception of protocol for XF understandings of reproductive sovereignty may not be immediately obvious. If 'protocol is a materialized functioning of distributed control',[63] then it would seem to be a particularly volatile tool for emancipatory gender politics, given that the meaning of a specific protocol will depend upon *what*, precisely, is being controlled in a given situation. Its object, along with its circumstances of enactment, will inevitably shape its resonances and feminist utility.

But as much as the protocol might represent a pervasive and equivocal means of control within network societies, it is nevertheless a tool to be annexed. Protocol logic can be repurposed and put to other ends – something Galloway and Thacker make clear in their discussion of 'counterprotocols'.[64] The 'first step in realizing an ethics and a politics of networks', they argue, is 'an activation of a political consciousness that is as capable of the critiquing of protocological control as it is capable of fostering the transformative elements of protocol'.[65] Fostering these transformative elements is one potential strut of a xenofeminist project – and crucially, as we shall see, may facilitate a better understanding of the concrete politics of scale. Let us further pursue this point by returning to our central case study.

The protocols around menstrual extraction – including where the procedure should take place, in what style and format information was communicated, and the level of involvement of the person undergoing the procedure – were laid out by the device's developers and by various local groups. As protocols, these guidelines were intended to be transmissible, and encouraged what feminist health activists believed to be best practice. This typically involved people narrating their experiences of the procedure and inserting their own specula, for example, and encouraged the framing of menstrual extraction as a group experience – a technique learned and performed among solidarity networks taking ownership of their collective health by experimenting on one another. This notion of the personal network was particularly important given the sensitive legal situation at the time.

Groups practising self-help (including menstrual extraction) 'were legally harassed, so most operated more or less underground'.[66] During that rather over-heated historical moment, the establishment of close-knit feminist collectives worked to reduce the risk of exposure, whilst the protocol permitted both practical instructions and political principles to flow beyond specific collectives with relative ease and safety. It was not simply that guidelines for procedural behaviours facilitated the preservation of closed networks and therefore reduced the risk of legal consequences. Crucially, these guidelines also allowed the self-help movement to reach beyond its initial instantiations and to enter new territories. Key ideas could be disseminated and passed on without quashing situational differences, thereby enabling self-help to exceed its various local contexts.

After all, as Galloway and Thacker remark, the protocol represents a bridge between autonomous agents, and, as such, speaks to the possibility of translocal operations. Its qualities of both relationality and adaptability help to ensure its pronounced capacity for *transmissibility*. As with memes, pliability enables transmission: the protocol can evolve to suit specific contexts, whilst retaining sufficient determining characteristics to remain more or less recognizably itself. A given protocol can therefore feasibly preserve a great deal of its influential and organizational capacity, both through and despite its potential mobility. The protocol, as we have conceived of it here, is the tractable and vigorous directional force within an open system, and a tool for training order 'to emerge as an "invisible hand"' from apparent spontaneity'.[67] Menstrual extraction's protocols (like *OBOS*) could be made subject to strategic appropriation via recontextualization. In this sense, the modifiable community norms surrounding its use can be seen as another example of the Del-Em's (re)purposeful activities. This returns us to the question of scale.

Murphy claims that menstrual extraction, as practised by members of the second-wave feminist self-help health movement, was 'a biopolitical project simultaneously on a microscale and macroscale. The microbiopolitical effort sought to technically create individualized control over the sexed reproductive body, while the macrobiopolitical register was traced by the flexible, universalizable, and mobile features of a protocol intended to bind and circulate among women in aggregate anywhere and everywhere.'[68] The protocol itself was designed as a way of transiting between these two scales of political intent, the local and the global. This focus on scalability – on strategies for rolling out and transmitting political ideas via the protocol – offers an insight into how feminist activisms of the period attempted, however imperfectly, to engage with what I have elsewhere called the *mesopolitical*.[69] The mesopolitical operates between atomized, hyper-local interventions at the level of, for example, individual embodiment (micropolitics), on the one hand, and big-picture, speculative projects premised on the wholesale overthrowal of power at the level of the state or beyond (macropolitics), on the other.

Both of these tendencies – which dominate many elements of leftist discourse – can seem oblivious to material conditions on the ground and disinterested in identifying viable pathways to change. The mesopolitical is neglected within academic political philosophizing in part because it is so difficult to theorize outside of its concrete materializations. It is lived, situational, perpetually negotiated, and difficult to distil down to abstract principles; this is the scale of the everyday reproductive labour of the left. In the abstract, it can perhaps be characterized by a handful of rather broad principles – capacity building and outward-looking praxis; an appreciation of the transversality of oppression; solidarity with the emancipatory self-directed organizing of others; and a willingness to engage with 'rhizomatic connections among [. . .] resistances and

insubordinations'.[70] Without sufficient attention to the mesopolitical, the difficult work of
alliance building and of increasing the reach of
political ideas is too often left unconsidered. It is
within this context that the example of self-help
becomes particularly illuminating, given that the
protocol might be considered a specifically mesopolitical tactic.

But even as we consider what the protocol
might offer us, and how it could be appropriated
as a pragmatic move for scaling up our own gender-political projects, we must remain attentive
to its limitations. As with many other valuable
emancipatory interventions, it is not sufficient in
and of itself – something that those within the
self-help movement, not to mention their critics,
were quick to recognize. The actual applications
of the Del-Em, along with the protocols surrounding its use, were just one node in a wider
network of efforts for long-term transformation
that emerged through the movement. Several
of these efforts produced particularly tenacious
forms of change which proved difficult for oppos-
ing forces to disembed. For example, activists
(including Rothman) made efforts to 'establish
a new medical infrastructure'.[71] This involved

not only working to establish discrete health-care facilities across California, but also efforts to spread the project into new areas. Throughout the 1970s, the founders of the self-help movement contributed to a National Federation of Feminist Women's Health Centers, which linked up feminist organizations across the US in the hopes of securing further gains for reproductive sovereignty and bodily autonomy.

Elsewhere, feminist action for health utilized an ecology of activisms to simultaneously facilitate change at multiple sites and scales. Whilst Jane might be seen as having practised a sticking-plaster approach to managing individual reproductive crisis – taking action that 'might help a few women but did not further or reflect the social changes' other feminist organizations envisioned[72] – it also informally affiliated with different groups to push for legislative change. Jane cooperated with the Clergy Consultation Service on Abortion, for example – a Baptist group that not only offered a referral service, but worked 'overtly for legalized abortion and educate[d] people about the issue. Their cloak of moral authority allowed them to take a public stand' when other groups could not.[73]

These examples point to the various strata of the mesopolitical: from protocols within and across closed groups, to the formalizing of these protocols via public-facing facilities, to the federalizing of these same facilities, to coalition and cooperation with distinct organizations. All of these political technologies have potential tactical value in terms of building a broad-based, issue-driven movement, and the legislative and infrastructural gains that pro-choice feminist health activism fostered in the seventies have enjoyed both reach and longevity, even in the face of repeated challenges from the religious right.[74]

Despite evidence of an attentiveness to scalability, however, many of the forms of activism we have been discussing in this chapter remain markedly restricted in terms of their scope and ambition. I am thinking particularly here about their narrow understanding of 'the right to choose', conceptualized primarily in terms of access to abortion. We must not frame reproductive sovereignty as a single-issue struggle. Feminists of colour have long stressed the necessity of a holistic understanding of 'choice', with the reproductive justice movement explicitly combining agitation for reproductive rights with engagement around wider social issues. Proponents of reproductive justice have eschewed a tight focus on fertility control in favour of building networks of solidarity around housing, employment, child care, and many other issues – all of which impact upon the ability to exercise meaningful choice.

As we have seen throughout this text, a truly emancipatory gender politics needs to think beyond *biological* reproduction and extend more thoroughly towards *social* reproduction (a point that activists of colour have been careful to stress). So far, our discussion has touched upon how the self-help movement reached out to other pro-choice organizations, but it has yet to challenge the understanding of choice upon which such a framing relies. On this note, I would like to address one final point of resonance between the Del-Em and the idea of a xenofeminist technology – that is, its (partial and potential) intersectional applicability.

## Technologies That Travel: Intersectional Applications

Menstrual extraction, as a practice combining technological devices with politicized interpersonal interactions, was explicitly developed to reach different contexts and constituencies, via the sharable yet adaptable protocol. As we have seen, the character of these protocols was deliberately flexible (that is, open to repurposing), and the terms under which groups used the Del-Em could be customized according to preference and need. Such protocol feminism was 'inventive of practices, manuals, and guidelines that could move translocally and that explicitly sought to take note of how power, emotion, and bonding circulated within clinical settings so as to create less oppressive medical experiences and less pathologizing research'.[75] Reproductive healthcare and fertility control, thus framed, were viewed as having the potential to cut across lines of class, race, ability, and so on – and, indeed, the Del-Em did manage to exceed its largely white, middle-class context of invention. The device played a documented role in Black feminist health initiatives: for example, the National Black Women's Health Project in the US provided information on menstrual extraction via its in-house magazine,[76] and included it as a topic at its annual Wellness Conference.

There are numerous reasons why such a technology might appeal to feminists of colour. As

Angela Davis suggests, noting the unequal distribution of deaths prior to 1973, Black and Puerto Rican people were 'far more familiar than their white sisters with the murderously clumsy scalpels of inept abortionists seeking profit in illegality'.[77] Finding safer forms of abortion was a priority for these groups, and, indeed, 'close to half of all the legal abortions' immediately following the passage of *Roe v. Wade* were received by people of colour.[78] However, given that the National Black Women's Health Project continued to discuss menstrual extraction and the Del-Em some decades after the *Roe v. Wade* decision, it is apparent that legal access and increased regulation of providers were not the only factors motivating feminists of colour to look towards self-help. Certainly the passage of the Hyde amendment in 1977 which 'prohibited the use of federal Medicaid funds to pay for abortion except when the life of the mother is at risk'[79] triggered a wave of changes at the state level that made abortion less financially accessible to many. For those receiving public assistance (significant numbers of whom were people of colour), such changes reasserted the need to be able to circum-navigate official legal and medical channels of reproductive healthcare.

But even if abortion *was* financially and legally accessible, there were still reasons for people to seek out other ways of meeting their needs. I am thinking particularly here of the disproportionately raced occurrences of non-consensual sterilization in the twentieth century, but we might also consider the exploitation of non-white bodies in medical testing, attempts to impose long-term contraceptives such as Norplant and Depo-Provera upon welfare recipients, and other forms of racist, classist, and cissexist disciplining of bodies.[80] Given the compound oppressions that non-white subjects endure when negotiating healthcare (in North America and elsewhere), it is easy to grasp why activists would argue both for the importance of a more inclusive and representative medical profession *and* for better ways in which to circumnavigate this profession altogether. The potential usefulness of a technology like the Del-Em transcends the limited context in which it was developed, and (as we have seen) the use of attendant protocols helps to encourage this transcendence by fostering context-sensitive adaptation.

However, a truly intersectional self-help activism would not be satisfied with claiming menstrual extraction's applicability beyond its original user base. This is something that many activists were well aware of. Ehrenreich and English, for example, note that

> it would be naive to assume that, because all women experience medical sexism, all women have the same needs and priorities at this time. Class differences in the medical treatment of women may not be as sharp as they were eighty years ago, but they are still very real. For black women, medical racism often overshadows medical sexism. For poor women of all ethnic groups, the problem of how to get services of any kind often overshadows all qualitative concerns.[81]

As they neatly put it, 'A movement that recognizes our biological similarity but denies the diversity of our priorities cannot be a women's health movement, it can only be *some women's* health movement.'[82] Indeed, feminists of colour have been clear in their message that health activism must be about more than fertility control, and have done a great deal to steer the discourse on reproduction in a more thorough, nuanced, and wide-ranging direction.

Davis, for example, notes that 'Birth control – individual choice, safe contraceptive methods, as well as abortion when necessary – is a fundamental prerequisite for the emancipation of women.'[83] However, whilst the 'progressive potential of birth control remains indisputable',[84] the history of feminist activism leaves 'much to be desired in the realm of challenges to racism and class exploitation'.[85] As she puts it,

> If the abortion rights campaign of the early 1970s needed to be reminded that women of color wanted desperately to escape the back-room quack abortionists, they should have also realized that these same women were not about to express pro-abortion statements. They were in favor of abortion rights, which did not mean that they were proponents of abortion. When Black and Latina women resort to abortions in such large numbers, the stories they tell are not so much about their desire to be free of their pregnancy, but rather about the miserable social conditions which dissuade them from bringing new lives into the world.[86]

As this quote indicates, the work of indigenous activists and feminists of colour has been crucial in ensuring that issues of social reproduction are not separated out from those of biological reproduction in our conception of what meaningful choice looks like.

The idea of self-help 'connotes some very different meanings' when used within differently raced contexts.[87] Within the predominately white women's health movement, it tends to refer to a limited range of practices involved in asserting agency over reproduction, including the use of specific medical technologies (the speculum, the Del-Em, and so on). Within the Black women's health movement, self-help is more likely to also include the activation of networks of community support and solidarity in relation to a wider range of issues – housing provision, employment, child care, police violence, and (as the previous chapter gestured towards) access to air, water, and other resources that are not damagingly toxic. Intersectional understandings of reproductive justice, then, should not be reduced to efforts to ensure the legal provision of abortion or contraception.

As Jennifer Nelson puts it, 'Demands to satisfy basic needs cannot be separated from reproductive politics, because a right to reproductive control is hollow without a right to live free of hunger, racism, and violence and without the dignity that facilitates real choices for one's own future and community.'[88] The SisterSong network – with which the National Black Women's Health Project is affiliated – is one example of the important work being done in this area. On its website, SisterSong states that: 'Abortion access is critical, and women of color and other marginalized women also often have difficulty accessing: contraception, comprehensive sex education, STI prevention and care, alternative birth options, adequate prenatal and pregnancy care, domestic violence assistance, adequate wages to support our families, safe homes, and so much more.'[89] Its proposed strategies seek to address the network of power relations underpinning this fusion of issues, and recognize reproductive justice as 'an opportunity and a call to come together as one movement with the power to win freedom for all oppressed people'.[90] Thus framed, reproductive justice becomes the basis of a mass movement with genuinely intersectional applicability.

If this potential is to be recognized, we must persistently embrace a more holistic concept of reproductive justice. Such a characterization is necessary to ensure that protocols are not unwittingly limited to the concerns of middle-class, able-bodied, white, cishet women. Reproductive justice is as much about support for having and raising children in conditions of safety and freedom as it is about resisting personally unwanted births. Medical instruments, their protocols, and the gendered anatomy towards which they are directed should not be considered the universal kernel of feminist self-help, with socio-political issues of particular constituencies positioned as appendages or optional extras. Instead, we must see technologies like the Del-Em as helpful but partial implements within a wider assemblage of structures, bodies, social relations, and material artefacts. This is a lesson that xenofeminism must bear in mind if it wishes to be a meaningfully coalitional project – that is, if it truly seeks to be 'a ready-to-hand tool for multiple political bodies and something that can be appropriated against the numerous oppressions that transect with gender and sexuality'.[91]

Crucially, SisterSong's approach to reproductive justice is vocally and explicitly trans* inclusive. Its website points out that 'Indigenous women, women of color, and trans* people have always fought for Reproductive Justice.'[92] Members recently hosted a Twitter discussion on the topic of 'queering reproductive justice', highlighting that the collective's activist framework extends to things like access to hormones, the right to use one's bathroom of preference, and advocacy for sex workers. Despite (as I remarked earlier) the feminism of the second wave sometimes manifesting itself in trans* exclusionary forms, the work of SisterSong illustrates that there are nevertheless characteristics of the self-help movement that can be reclaimed and extended to the technomaterialist transfeminist projects of today. Indeed, it is perhaps within the realm of biotechnologies that we can detect particularly productive intergenerational connections between feminist projects that might otherwise seem attitudinally different.

In the final section, I want to trace the connections between the feminist health movement of the 1970s and more recent interventions around trans* health issues. Whilst I do not have the space to explore these entanglements in great detail here, I hope to at least point to some broad coordinates of confluence and resonance. This strikes me as particularly important given recent interventions that pit these forms of activism against each other, particularly contextualizing gains for the LGBTQIA* community in relation to losses for some feminist or pro-choice positions.[93] By stressing the shared commitments of these movements, I hope to demonstrate that this tendency is unnecessarily hostile and divisive, whilst continuing to articulate an expanded understanding of self-help (as a protocol-driven practice, engaged in by a network of collectives, with the potential to go beyond a single-issue struggle).

## From Self-Help to Transfeminism

The first step in rethinking the legacies of second-wave feminist self-help practices is to resituate them in the context of their wider influences. Feminist health activism did not emerge from the minds of figures like Rothman fully formed, and nor was it solely the product of the women's movement; 'neighbourhood health clinics, grounded in the civil rights and New Left movements, provided intellectual, political, and practical experiential precedents for the women's health movement'.[94] Self-help had to actively *forget* its indebtedness to other kinds of activism in order to decentre race and class within its analysis; the situated knowledges of those dominant within the movement crowded out other ways of thinking about reproductive choice.

Following the model of reproductive justice, any xenofeminist approach must emphasize that the 'Y' in 'DIY' never operates in isolation, but is enmeshed in a web of structural oppressions, networks of power, and technomaterial relationships. XF must insist upon conceiving of political agency as necessarily collective, and therefore upon emancipatory politics as openly and inherently coalitional. Given that a seemingly oblivious cis-sexism characterized self-help just as much as its unwitting racism (in the form of particular lacunas that stymied its ambitions to provide a service to every feminist), it is important that we finish by looking more closely at how we might effectively strip the second wave for parts, so as to take what it can offer (and has already given) to queer and trans* activism, whilst discarding that which is unhelpful. This in itself might be positioned as a practice of repurposing, and therefore as in accordance with a xenofeminist politics of technology.

One vital link in the chain between second-wave self-help and contemporary work on queer and trans* healthcare is the HIV/AIDS activism of the 1980s and 1990s – particularly that undertaken by the Women's Caucus of ACT UP. In their book *Women, AIDS and Activism*, members of the Caucus acknowledge their debts to the feminist health movement, remarking that 'People with AIDS must become experts about their bodies, HIV treatments, and wellness maintenance. This mode of empowerment through knowledge harks back to the women's self-help health movement of the 1970s.'[95] In the authors' opinion, reproductive justice and AIDS activism are intimately connected, not only via their shared emphasis on increasing agency through knowledge, but also thanks to a common attention to sexual pleasure, and because those with a positive diagnosis encounter particular challenges with regard to reproductive rights.

The cyberfeminist group subRosa is amongst those who have remarked upon affinities between these two forms of political engagement, linking this to more recent developments in healthcare activism and dissident embodiment. It notes that

the tactical activists of ACT-UP contested the medical system and its treatment of the HIV and

AIDS crisis, and emerged as the direct successors of the Feminist Health Movement though broadening its strategies and concerns. Within the last decade, another strong challenge to the medical establishment has come from genderqueer, transsex and intersex activists who are contending with biomedical and human rights and legal institutions in many different ways. The radical body interventions used in both freely chosen and coerced sexual and gender reassignment surgery and therapy can often involve procedures such as plastic and reconstructive surgery and psychological counseling, as well as genetic testing, hormone and drug therapies, stem cell and fertility technologies. Thus genderqueer people intersect with a wide array of medical, cultural, and disciplinary systems.[96]

The legacy of second-wave health activism can be felt in the transfeminist agitation of today, despite the fact that there is only limited evidence of the self-help movement catering to trans* people directly.[97] As subRosa's comments suggest, self-help has become mobile through appropriation; its ethos has been adopted but extended, its tactics repurposed by the health activists who practised in its wake.

Indeed, this is demonstrated in the changing relationship between trans* politics and the classic reference text of the feminist self-help movement, *OBOS*. We have already seen how this book was taken up and recontextualized by feminists outside of the Global North, and how this proliferation and repurposing ultimately changed the way the book circulated in the States. It has also been transformed in various ways by the attentions of the trans* community. For example, 2014 saw the publication of a phonebook-sized tome entitled *Trans Bodies, Trans Selves: A Resource for the Transgender Community* (*TBTS*). This text was explicitly inspired by *OBOS*, and makes direct reference to it at several points. The collection even concludes with an afterword by the Boston Women's Health Book Collective, in which the group acknowledges the deficiencies of its earlier work in terms of addressing trans* issues.

The authors remark that thanks to *TBTS* and 'all the transgender folks who have been writing and teaching over the past many years, we, a group of cisgender women, now know that we can no longer say "a women's body" and mean only one thing'.[98] They then proceed to identify a range of issues around which a more properly intersectional health activism might be assembled. These include fuller access to reproductive health screening – the Pap test, for example, is 'recommended for people of any gender who have a cervix' – and advocacy in terms of making hormones safer to use.[99] The text as a whole provides verified, accessibly written, and wide-ranging information, from contributors who are themselves transgender or genderqueer. As such, it seeks to provide a quality-assured self-help resource to its trans* readers.

Of course, *TBTS* is unlikely to achieve the prominence of its seventies predecessor, in part because the internet has so thoroughly transformed the manner in which information about gendered embodiment and reproductive health is located. As Susan Stryker notes in *Transgender History*, self-published materials such as paper-based newsletters and zines became much less ubiquitous in the second half of the 1990s, their 'numbers and frequency [dropping] off precipitously in the middle of the decade in reverse proportion to the rise of the Internet age'.[100] With the arrival of user-friendly web browsers such as Netscape Navigator, the internet became 'a cheaper distribution outlet than even the cheapest paper-based, surface-mailed publications – and once the first generation of search engines made finding online content as easy as typing a search term, one capable of reaching vast potential audiences'.[101] From the mid-nineties onwards, tailored resources emerged online to serve trans* communities: early examples included *Susan's Place*, which started as a chat room in 1995; *Transsexual and Transgender Road Map*, launched in 1996; and a range of other bulletin boards and virtual community groups.

These sites enabled people to engage in information sharing, and to better connect for the purposes of coordinated self-advocacy and mutual peer support. Those on the receiving end of medical care were no longer simply the object of a closed discussion internal to the medical-industrial complex, but positioned as active subjects, collectively negotiating their own care and their relationships with providers. As Stryker puts it, the 'remarkable expansion of the transgender movement in the mid-1990s would not have been possible without the Internet's even more remarkable and rapid transformation of the means of mass communication'.[102] This is not to suggest that the advent of the internet instantly eradicated all barriers to accessing high-quality health and wellbeing data: information initially remained dispersed and sometimes difficult to find, and was frequently incomplete or inaccurate – and, of course, the digital divide meant that access to this brave new world was extremely uneven. However, the days of borrowing library cards from friendly medical students were swiftly becoming a thing of the past. The DIY spirit of any *OBOS*-style intervention in the digital age is, I would argue, better reflected in the forums of the nineties or the online communities of today than it is in a print publication released by Oxford University Press. Today, trans\* people who cannot or do not wish to consult a medical professional are arguably far more likely to turn to Google or to a subreddit for answers than they are to consult a self-help book.

However, the connections between contemporary trans\* activism and seventies self-help remain very much apparent. Whilst these connections tend to be overlooked – particularly in celebratory appraisals of the second wave – a handful of critics have addressed the evident common ground between them. Lauren Porsch, for example, argues that the transgender health movement followed a similar trajectory to that underpinning 1970s self-help: 'negative health care encounters, which run the gamut from provider ignorance and insensitivity, to purposeful humiliation, to the actual denial of care' have resulted in collective organizing to 'empower the transgender community to advocate for their own needs in the health care setting'.[103] Emi Koyama similarly insists upon the fact that transfeminism emphasizes the profound connections between trans* emancipation and the rights for the impregnatable, partly because both depend on ideas of self-determination and gendered embodiment: 'like women seeking an abortion, our bodies have become an open territory, a battleground'.[104]

Adopting a reproductive justice perspective, Koyama stresses that 'choice is also about resisting the coerced sterilization or abortion of less privileged women. Likewise, transfeminism strives for the right to refuse surgical and hormonal interventions, including those prescribed for intersex people.'[105] Clearly this inclusive framework is appropriate for coalitional transfeminist activism, given the need to more fully appreciate the fusion of structural oppressions many trans* people encounter (in terms of race, class, immigration status, sexuality, and so on). The insufficiency of a narrow focus on conventional healthcare is particularly obvious when we concentrate upon the needs of poor trans* communities of colour; after all, whilst trans* health and wellbeing can and does incorporate hormone therapy, breast and chest health, reproductive health screenings, pregnancy care, and so on, it must also extend to protection from violence, homicide prevention, and material action to make all trans* lives more liveable.

In this chapter, I have used a specific case study – namely, the Del-Em and the technomaterial relations surrounding its development – as a means via which to explore what a xenofeminist technology might look like. In the process, I have fleshed out four key principles: the circumnavigation of gatekeepers; repurposing; scalability; and intersectionality. Ultimately, my case study has underscored the necessity of adopting a more comprehensive approach to reproduction – one that goes beyond biological procreation to confront wider social conditions, but without losing sight of the body as a potential locus of emancipatory endeavour. In the brief conclusion that follows, I will expand this analysis, turning to more recent interventions in gendered embodiment. Where does xenofeminist technopolitics go from here?

# Conclusion: Xeno-Reproduction

In this book, I have attempted to conceptualize xenofeminist principles in relation to the theme of reproduction. Chapter 1 used Firestone's work on assistive reproductive technologies and cybernetic communism to articulate a tripartite definition of XF – one grounded in ideas of technomaterialism, anti-naturalism, and gender abolitionism. By framing these three key characteristics in relation to Firestone's work, and by emphasizing their connection with both biological and social reproduction, we came to understand how they might function together within a single emancipatory project. In Chapter 2, we considered the relationship between reproduction and futurity via a discussion of contemporary eco-activisms.

We focused on the figure of the Child as an icon of the perpetuation of racist, heteronormative class values, whilst problematizing any supposedly forward-looking radical politics based on 'biopolitical border control' and the prevention of future births. Kin making was understood here as a reorientation of genetic and non-genetic bonds alike – a privileging of xeno-hospitality over and against both population control and naturalized reproductive futurism.

The final chapter extended this discussion to feminist technologies. We used the example of a single reproductive 'handcraft tool' (and the social relations surrounding and constituting it) to help elaborate an XF politics of collective autonomy, repurposing, scalability, and intersectionality. Our analysis concluded by insisting upon the importance of transfeminist reproductive justice frameworks, and by pointing to potential vectors of solidarity between the self-help and trans* health movements. Encouragingly – and relevantly, given Chapter 3's discussion of menstrual extraction – it seems that attempts to foster just this kind of solidarity are emerging around technomaterial projects today. I want to conclude this book by gesturing towards a number of initiatives that, in one way or another, resonate with XF ambitions.

I would argue that we can see the potential inheritances of a device such as the Del-Em being played out within the grassroots feminism of the GynePunk collective – a group that puts into practice some of the ideas with which xenofeminism grapples in theory. GynePunk taps into the energy of queer activism, biohacking, and the maker movement to design free and open source hardware for self-diagnosis and care. The group helped develop 3D-printed specula for the auto-administration of Pap smears, for example, and assembles functional DIY lab equipment from technological detritus such as discarded hard-drive motors and webcams – requisitioning mundane material artefacts in a manner clearly reminiscent of the design history of the Del-Em.[1] In addition to helping under-served communities (including sex workers, migrants, and trans* people) to circumnavigate medical gatekeepers, the GynePunk project espouses a positive ethos of corporeal self-experimentation. It views the body as 'a technology to be hacked, from the established ideas of gender and sex, to exploring the capacity to start researching ourselves, to find our own ideas and technologies, to help us be free, autonomous and independent from the system'.[2]

GynePunk's activities are largely in keeping with those of feminist self-help. The project represents '*Our Bodies, Ourselves* updated for a digitalized and globalized world',[3] and has been compared to the work of Jane in the 1970s.[4] Indeed, GynePunk appears to be deliberately aligning itself with the heritage of the women's health movement when it refers to its members as 'cyborg witches'.[5] The witch – a figure seen by second-wave feminists as an exemplar of repressed knowledges and appropriated expertise – is here upgraded for the twenty-first century via hybridization with a wider range of technological devices. It is the group's 'view of the body as a technology and their invention of new and DIY diagnostic tools that marks them as cyborgs; their reclamation of ancestral women's knowledge around reproductive health that marks them as witches'.[6]

Within GynePunk's breed of cyborg witchcraft, it is not just devices and their constitutive parts that are available for deliberate repurposing, but bodies and ideologies as well. The hallmarks of the feminist health activisms of the seventies are augmented here by a renewed attention to the mutability of biological materiality, extending to reproductive embodiment and gender itself. The result is a technologically literate, (re)purposeful feminism that addresses itself to people's specific health needs rather than to a naturalized idea of dichotomous gender. This is a vast improvement over potentially exclusionary second-wave discourses of 'women's health in women's hands' – a shift that renders self-help far more hospitable to xenofeminism's gender abolitionist approach.

Other interventions emerging from within a renewed (and newly queered) feminist self-help tradition include Ryan Hammond's *Open Source Gender Codes* (*OSGC*) project – an initiative seeking to further bridge the gap between self-help healthcare and the free and open source software movement. In a move partially inspired by Preciado's work, as well as by the xenofeminist manifesto itself, Hammond engages with contemporary biohacking practices in an effort to imagine new ways of disseminating medical technologies. *OSGC* seeks to enable people to grow their own hormones at dedicated community hubs using transgenic tobacco plants – a

species chosen for its 'proven ability to manu-
facture pharmaceutically valuable molecules'.[7]
The development of a transgenic plant that
'could allow "laypeople" to grow sex hormones
would not only call into question the cultural and
institutional frameworks that govern queer and
trans bodies, it would also challenge the current
system of pharmaceutical production. Can we
imagine a communal system of pharmaceutical
production in which biological materials are collectively owned?'[8] In the spirit of 1970s self-help,
*OSGC* seeks to develop an accessible method of
producing biotechnologies that can evade gatekeepers and, with them, healthcare profiteering
and oppressive forms of pathologization. As such,
it can be seen as a move against the further enclosure of a once-collective knowledge base, and as
another example of queer cyborgian witchcraft.

These projects add a concrete dimension to
debates about what a xenofeminist technology
might look like. An important caveat before I
conclude, however: our discussions here and in
Chapter 3 have largely focused on technologies
as a means of helping gendered subjects carve
out a space of autonomy within disciplinary
systems that remain difficult to navigate, both

materially and politically. As such, much of our analysis has positioned these tools (from menstrual extraction, to self-performed diagnostic testing, to grow-your-own hormones) as defensive technologies – that is, as means to promote collective agency over gender and reproductive embodiment when access to professional care is somehow limited. For all its XF possibilities, something like the Del-Em is at best a pragmatic and transitional device. Instead of accepting the circumnavigation of gatekeepers as an endpoint for xenofeminist action, and celebrating the tools that enable this, it is beholden upon us to devise ways of extending the project's reach.

It is not enough to think about routing around barriers; in order to ensure maximal emancipatory gains, we must facilitate the creation of new systems. As we remark in the manifesto, from 'the global to the local, from the cloud to our bodies, xenofeminism avows the responsibility in constructing new institutions of technomaterialist hegemonic proportions'.[9] We must be engineers as well as hackers, conceiving of 'a total structure as well as the molecular parts from which it is constructed'.[10] This means leveraging the tactic of the protocol in search of more efficient ways to scale, and engaging an ecology of activisms that may be better suited to bridging the micro-, meso-, and macropolitical levels of our complex technomaterial world. Developments such as GynePunk and *OSGC* predominantly focus on workarounds rather than on re-engineering biotechnical hegemony. Both projects remain dependent upon the wider medical infrastructure as it stands.

Just as Jane's Pap smear service came to rely on a conventional lab for cytology in the early 1970s, so too is GynePunk's focus on the participatory (anti)clinic somewhat restricted, limited as it is to sample collection and basic diagnostics. Likewise, traditional technoscientific settings remain crucial to *OSGC*. Hammond can aspire to 'bring the queer community into the lab' and to 'bring the lab to queer communities',[11] but must continue to rely on established outsourced systems at both ends of the envisioned DIY process. In order to successfully develop transgenic tobacco plants, *OSGC* requires controlled conditions and access to scientific resources that are at present largely privatized. Should the development of the plants be successful, and a grow-your-own hormone system become implementable without regulatory strictures, existing infrastructure would still be required for post-processing (including extraction, purification, and dosage activities).

Once again, we see both the difficulty and the necessity of scaling up those interventions that take the individual body as their starting point; somewhere down the line, established techno-material conditions and the medical-industrial complex will reassert themselves. The disruptive practices of DIY gender hacking need to be complemented by broader attempts to ensure extensive and enduring change (an area in which 1970s self-help was intermittently successful) – to reconfigure not only specific bodies and subjectivities, but also the far-reaching institutional formations of the technomaterial world. A transfeminist health movement that seeks to be 'proportionate to the monstrous complexity of our reality' must position itself as part of a wider anti-racist, anti-imperialist, anti-capitalist struggle.[12] As with the reproductive justice framework, we must trace the multiple entanglements of health beyond atomized bodies, medical conditions, and corporeal states into the interconnected network of oppressions and privileges that systematically shape all forms of embodied experience.

None of this is to deny the necessity of contemporary, technologically mediated self-help projects. The initiatives I have touched upon here all speak, in various interesting and important ways, to particular xenofeminist concerns. To remind oneself of their limitations is to remind oneself of the potential boundaries of XF as a whole – the internal tensions between its communism and its anarchism; its dual focus on big-picture counter-hegemonic projects and small-scale, decentralized interventions; its oscillation between the human and the posthuman. Whilst one xenofeminist mode celebrates resistance through repurposing, another points to appropriation itself as an indicator of disempowerment – a disruption from within a system that continues to be stacked against us; a moment of cunning, potentially capable of achieving specific ends, but by no means an unqualified good in itself. The challenge, as I have suggested elsewhere in this book, is to think mesopolitically – a task for which an emphasis on both coalitional praxis and thinking through protocols may provide helpful resources.

Arguably, the contemporary projects we have discussed here *do* attempt to engage with infrastructural change to a greater or lesser extent. Both gesture towards the wider promise of synthetic biology as a means of undermining the patent system, for example (though neither has taken Rothman's approach of strategically appropriating intellectual property law to secure a technology's free circulation into the future). However, there is a great deal more to be done, and we need to ensure that the labour of constructing mesopolitical transits is not allowed to slip from view. The ultimate aim of a xenofeminist politics of technology should be to transform political systems and disciplinary structures themselves, so that autonomy does not always have to be craftily, covertly, and repeatedly seized (given that the requirement of such seizure, if imposed upon an unwilling subject, takes the form of a burden rather than an emancipatory exercise of freedom).

To reiterate the point, repurposing must be viewed as a step towards more durable forms of transformation. This includes the gradual construction of better forms of (always contingent, always provisional) technomaterial hegemony, in which we do not always have to start from the need to appropriate things – to turn them radically against their original purposes – because they were in fact *designed* with a more accommodating set of affordances in mind. Technological repurposing may speak to survival pending revolution (part of a dissident form of social reproduction that acts as the very underpinning of all possible change). However, ensuring the provision of safer, cheaper, fully accessible gender-disruptive and reproductive healthcare should be our priority. I am grateful to have second-wave self-help to appropriate and learn from, but ultimately we need to construct alternative models for xeno-reproduction.

# Notes

## Introduction

1 Laboria Cuboniks, 'Xenofeminism: A Politics for Alienation', 2015 (http://www.laboriacuboniks.net).
2 Academic influences include Rosi Braidotti, Wendy Hui Kyong Chun, Evelyn Fox Keller, Sarah Kember, Lisa Nakamura, and Judy Wajcman. These thinkers deserve a prominent place in the genealogies of XF and contemporary technofeminism, as I have tried to stress elsewhere: see A. Avanessian and H. Hester (eds), *Dea ex Machina*, trans. Jennifer Sophia Theodor (Berlin: Merve, 2015). Perhaps the most obvious voices omitted from the current discussion are those of pre-millennial cyberfeminists – people who are not only some of Laboria Cuboniks' most significant predecessors but also, in several cases, our ongoing collaborators and peers. This includes members of the 90s cyber-collectives VNS Matrix, the Old Boys Network,

subRosa, and the Cybernetic Cultures Research Unit (most notably, Sadie Plant). In side-lining explicit engagement with such figures, I am in no way seeking to downplay their influence upon the manifesto. Indeed, I have directly addressed the connection between 90s cyberfeminism and contemporary xenofeminist tendencies in other publications: see H. Hester, 'After the Future: *n* Hypotheses of Post-Cyber Feminism', *Res Gallery: The Kathy Rae Huffman Archive Catalogue* (http://beingres.org/2017/06/30/afterthefuture-helen-hester/). I would urge readers to look beyond this little book to develop a more representative understanding of XF.

## Chapter 1   What is Xenofeminism?

1  S. Firestone, *The Dialectic of Sex: The Case for Feminist Revolution* (London: Women's Press, 1979), 163.
2  Ibid., 182.
3  Laboria Cuboniks, 'Xenofeminism'.
4  N. K. Hayles, *How We Became Posthuman: Virtual Bodies in Cybernetics, Literature, and Informatics* (Chicago: University of Chicago Press, 1999), 18.
5  Laboria Cuboniks, 'Xenofeminism'.
6  Firestone, *Dialectic*, 193.
7  Ibid., 190.
8  S. Franklin, 'Revisiting Reprotech: Firestone and the Question of Technology', in M. Merck and S. Sandford (eds), *The Further Adventures of The Dialectic of Sex: Critical Essays on Shulamith Firestone* (Basingstoke: Palgrave, 2010), 41.

9 Ibid., 34.

10 J. Wajcman, *Feminism Confronts Technology* (Cambridge: Polity, 1991), 23.

11 Laboria Cuboniks, 'Xenofeminism'.

12 Firestone, *Dialectic*, 188.

13 Ibid., 213.

14 Franklin, 'Revisiting Reprotech', 31.

15 M. Mies and V. Shiva, 'Introduction: Why We Wrote This Book Together', in Mies and Shiva, *Ecofeminism* (London: Zed Books, 1993), 16.

16 M. Mies, 'White Man's Dilemma: His Search For What He Has Destroyed', in Mies and Shiva, *Ecofeminism*, 138.

17 Ibid., 138–9.

18 Ibid., 139.

19 Ibid., 140.

20 Ibid., 139.

21 Laboria Cuboniks, 'Xenofeminism'.

22 I have no wish to diminish the trauma attached to many experiences of reproductive technologies or medicalized childbirth. As Firestone herself noted, under conditions of global capitalism, technologized reproduction will tend towards the nightmarish rather than the hopeful (as many of the circumstances surrounding transnational surrogacy suggest). We must nevertheless insist that there is nothing *inherently* masculinist, patriarchal, or discriminatory about science in itself. It is both a territory for and a means of enacting emancipatory anti-naturalist struggles.

23 Laboria Cuboniks, 'Xenofeminism'.

24 D. Haraway, *Modest_Witness@Second_Millennium. FemaleMan©_Meets_OncoMouse™: Feminism and Technoscience* (New York: Routledge, 1997), 62.

25 E. A. Wilson, *Gut Feminism* (Durham, NC: Duke University Press, 2015), 9.

26 Ibid., 45.

27 Ibid., 120.

28 See C. Waldby and M. Cooper, 'From Reproductive Work to Regenerative Labour: The Female Body and the Stem Cell Industries', *Feminist Theory*, 11(1) (2010), 3–22.

29 Firestone, *Dialectic*, 165.

30 N. Power, 'Toward a Cybernetic Communism: The Technology of the Anti-Family', in Merck and Sandford (eds), *Further Adventures*, 145.

31 Firestone, *Dialectic*, 183.

32 S. Sandford, 'The Dialectic of *The Dialectic of Sex*', in Merck and Sandford (eds), *Further Adventures*, 249.

33 Firestone, *Dialectic*, 11.

34 S. Stryker, *Transgender History* (Berkeley, CA: Seal Press, 2008), 108.

35 Ibid., 109.

36 In the UK, Sparkle – The National Transgender Charity sells t-shirts bearing the slogan 'trans* is not a choice: transphobia is!', whilst Trans Media Watch suggests that 'Most trans people feel they have no choice at all about how they live': 'Common Misunderstandings', 2013 (http://www.transmediawatch.org/misunderstandings.html).

37 Laboria Cuboniks, 'Xenofeminism'.

38  A. Escalante, 'Gender Nihilism: An Anti-Manifesto', *Libcom*, 22 June 2016 (https://libcom.org/library/gender-nihilism-anti-manifesto).

39  Laboria Cuboniks, 'Xenofeminism'.

40  Escalante, 'Gender Nihilism'.

41  Ibid.

42  Ibid.

43  In the case of race and class, discriminatory processes are not typically based on spontaneously occurring embodied differences – the colour of one's skin, for example, bears little relation to one's 'Natural' capacities, but is culturally over-coded with racist ideas of hierarchy. As such, the XF slogan 'If Nature is unjust, change Nature!' does not apply; the injustice stems not from Nature (as it is typically understood), but rather from deeply unequal social relations.

44  Laboria Cuboniks, 'Xenofeminism'.

45  Ibid.

46  Ibid.

47  Ibid.

48  subRosa, 'Useless Gender: An Immodest Proposal for Radical Justice', in *Yes Species* (Chicago: Sabrosa Books, 2005), 57.

49  M. Menon, *Indifference to Difference: On Queer Universalism* (Minneapolis: University of Minnesota Press, 2015), 41.

## Chapter 2  Xenofeminist Futurities

1  L. Edelman, *No Future: Queer Theory and the Death Drive* (Durham, NC: Duke University Press, 2004), 3.

2 Ibid., 19.

3 Ibid., 132.

4 Ibid., 75.

5 M. Mies, 'Mother Earth', in J. Hawley (ed.), *Why Women Will Save the Planet* (London: Zed Books, 2015), 178.

6 Ibid., 180.

7 k. butler and C. Raffensperger, 'The New Ecofeminism: Fulfilling Our Sacred Responsibilities to Future Generations', *Commons Magazine*, 7 August 2015 (http://www.onthecommons.org/magazine/the-new-ecofeminism#sthash.RygojCL5.v4vjb9YM.dpbs).

8 J. McConnell, 'Ecofeminism and the Future of Humanism', *Humanism Today*, 8 (1993), 113.

9 See Out of the Woods, 'The Future is Kids' Stuff', *Libcom*, 17 May 2015 (https://libcom.org/blog/future-kids-stuff-17052015).

10 N. Seymour, *Strange Natures: Futurity, Empathy, and the Queer Ecological Imagination* (Urbana: University of Illinois Press, 2013), viii.

11 Edelman, *No Future*, 2.

12 A. Gosine, 'Non-White Reproduction and Same-Sex Eroticism: Queer Acts Against Nature', in C. Mortimer-Sandilands and B. Erickson (eds), *Queer Ecologies: Sex, Nature, Politics, Desire* (Bloomington: Indiana University Press, 2010), 161.

13 Ibid., 158.

14 G. de Chiro, 'Polluted Politics? Confronting Toxic Discourse, Sex Panic, and Eco-Normativity', in Mortimer-Sandilands and Erickson (eds), *Queer Ecologies*, 201.

15 Indeed, mainstream anti-toxics activism appears to lean heavily on ideas of racialized (as well as queer) Otherness. Mel Chen points to twenty-first-century American media panics about lead paint in an analysis that neatly bridges reproductive futurity, environmental concerns, and discourses of race: 'lead's identity as a neurotoxic "heavy metal" was attributed to toys identified as made in China, toys whose decomposable surfaces when touched yielded up lead for transit into the bloodstreams of young children': 'Toxic Animacies, Inanimate Affections', *GLQ*, 17(2–3) (2011), 267.

16 T. Colborn, D. Dumanoski, and J. P. Myers, *Our Stolen Future: Are We Threatening Our Fertility, Intelligence, and Survival? A Scientific Detective Story* (New York: Dutton, 1996), 197.

17 Julian Gill-Peterson notes that the testosterone molecule 'circulates as a chemical index of environmental toxicity, one among countless drugs flushed through the industrial water system into rivers and oceans': 'The Technical Capacities of the Body: Assembling Race, Technology, and Transgender', *TSQ*, 1(3) (2014), 403. Eva Hayward, meanwhile, remarks upon how xenoestrogens 'found in foods, medicines, fertilizers, cosmetics, sanitary products, and other elements of material culture leak into habitats, environments, and ecosystems': 'Transxenoestrogenesis', *TSQ*, 1(1–2) (2014), 257.

18 M. Murphy, 'Distributed Reproduction', in M. J. Casper and P. Currah (eds), *Corpus: An Interdisciplinary Reader of Bodies and Knowledge* (Basingstoke: Palgrave, 2011), 33.

19  M. Ah-King and E. Hayward, 'Toxic Sexes: Perverting Pollution and Queering Hormone Disruption', *O-Zone: A Journal of Object-Oriented Studies*, 1(1) (2104), 5.

20  Di Chiro, 'Polluted Politics?', 208.

21  A. Shotwell, *Against Purity: Living Ethically in Compromised Times* (Minneapolis: University of Minnesota Press, 2016), 87.

22  Ibid., 93.

23  N. Power, 'Non-Reproductive Futurism: Rancière's Rational Equality Against Edelman's Body Apolitic', *Borderlands*, 8(2) (2009), 8.

24  Edelman, *No Future*, 156–7, n. 14.

25  See J. Nelson, *More Than Medicine: A History of the Feminist Women's Health Movement* (New York: New York University Press, 2015).

26  J. E. Muñoz, *Cruising Utopia: The Then and There of Queer Futurity* (New York: New York University Press, 2009), 94–5.

27  Ibid., 22.

28  Ibid., 96.

29  R. Sheldon, 'Reproductive Futurism and Feminist Rhetoric: Joanna Russ' *We Who Are about To . . .*', *Femspec*, 10(1) (2009), 19–35 (http://www.femspec.org/samples/sheldon.html).

30  D. Haraway, 'Anthropocene, Capitalocene, Plantationocene, Chthulucene: Making Kin', *Environmental Humanities*, 6 (2015), 161 (http://environmentalhumanities.org/arch/vol6/6.7.pdf).

31  United Nations Department of Social and Economic Affairs, 'World Population to Exceed 10 billion', 5 May

2011 (https://www.un.org/development/desa/en/news/
population/population-exceed-10-billion.html).

32 S. Hallegatte et al., *Shock Waves: Managing the Impacts
of Climate Change on Poverty* (Washington, DC:
World Bank Group, 2016), 4 (https://openknowledge.
worldbank.org/bitstream/handle/10986/22787/978146
4806735.pdf).

33 Haraway, 'Anthropocene', 162.

34 Ibid., 161.

35 Ibid.

36 Ibid., 162.

37 Edelman, *No Future*, 17.

38 M. Murphy, *Seizing the Means of Reproduction:
Entanglements of Feminism, Health, and Technoscience*
(Durham, NC: Duke University Press, 2012), 130.

39 M. Murphy, 'Economization of Life: Calculative
Infrastructures of Population and Economy', in
P. Rawes (ed.), *Relational Architectural Ecologies:
Architecture, Nature, and Subjectivity* (Abingdon:
Routledge, 2013), 146.

40 D. Haraway, 'Cyborgs for Earthly Survival!', *London
Review of Books: Letters*, 39(13), 29 June 2017 (https://
www.lrb.co.uk/v39/n13/letters).

41 S. Lewis, 'Cthulhu Plays No Role for Me', *Viewpoint
Magazine*, 8 May 2017 (https://www.viewpointmag.
com/2017/05/08/cthulhu-plays-no-role-for-me/).

42 A. Y. Davis, *Women, Race and Class* (New York:
Vintage Books, 1983), 215.

43 D. Haraway, *Staying with the Trouble: Making Kin
in the Chthulucene* (Durham, NC: Duke University
Press, 2016), 138.

44  Ibid., 138.

45  M. Puig de la Bellacasa, *Matters of Care: Speculative Ethics in More Than Human Worlds* (Minneapolis: University of Minnesota Press, 2017), 80.

46  Laboria Cuboniks, 'Xenofeminism'.

47  Ibid.

48  Haraway, *Staying with the Trouble*, 138.

49  R. Sheldon, *The Child to Come: Life After the Human Catastrophe* (Minneapolis: University of Minnesota Press, 2016), 5–6.

50  Ibid., 124.

51  Ibid., 29.

## Chapter 3    Xenofeminist Technologies

1  R. Rowan, 'Extinction as Usual? Geo-Social Futures and Left Optimism', *e-flux*, 31 July 2015 (http://supercommunity.e-flux.com/texts/extinction-as-usual-geo-social-futures-and-left-optimism/).

2  L. Kaplan, *The Story of Jane: The Legendary Underground Feminist Abortion Service* (New York: Pantheon Books, 1995), 197.

3  R. Chalker, 'Why Menstrual Extraction is a Good Idea', *On the Issues Magazine*, Spring 1993 (http://www.ontheissuesmagazine.com/1993spring/Spring1993_CHALKER2.php).

4  B. Ehrenreich and D. English, *Complaints and Disorders: The Sexual Politics of Sickness* (New York: Feminist Press, 2011), 156.

5  D. Haraway, *Simians, Cyborgs, and Women: The*

*Reinvention of Nature* (London: Free Association Press, 1991), 169.

6  T. Kapsalis, *Public Privates: Performing Gynecology from Both Ends of the Speculum* (Durham, NC: Duke University Press, 1997), 172.

7  Ibid., 168.

8  J. Wajcman, *Feminism Confronts Technology* (Cambridge: Polity, 1991), 17.

9  D. Haraway, 'The Virtual Speculum in the New World Order', in G. Kirkup, L. Janes, K. Woodward, and F. Hovenden (eds), *The Gendered Cyborg: A Reader* (London: Routledge, 2003), 237.

10  S. L. Vostral and D. McDonagh, 'A Feminist Inventor's Studio', in L. L. Layne, S. L. Vostral, and K. Boyer (eds), *Feminist Technology* (Urbana: University of Illinois Press, 2010), 200. Whilst some speculative ideas have been advanced in more recent years, the classic speculum design continues to dominate. See A. Pardes, 'The Speculum Finally Gets a Modern Redesign', *Wired*, 5 October 2017 (https://www.wired.com/story/the-speculum-finally-gets-a-modern-redesign/).

11  R. Eveleth, 'Why No One Can Design a Better Speculum', *The Atlantic*, 17 November 2014 (https://www.theatlantic.com/health/archive/2014/11/why-no-one-can-design-a-better-speculum/382534/).

12  Ehrenreich and English, *Complaints and Disorders*, 31.

13  Ibid., 35. Elements of this relationship persist to this day. As Chikako Takeshita remarks in her study of the IUD, doctors are still 'the ultimate gatekeepers of women's choices'. See C. Takeshita, *The Global Biopolitics of the IUD: How Science Constructs Contraceptive Users*

*and Women's Bodies* (Cambridge, MA: MIT Press, 2012), 103.

14 K. Davis, *The Making of Our Bodies, Ourselves: How Feminism Travels Across Borders* (Durham, NC: Duke University Press, 2007), 121.

15 Ibid.

16 Kaplan, *The Story of Jane,* ix–x.

17 Ibid., 130.

18 Ibid.

19 Ibid., xi.

20 Murphy, *Seizing the Means*, 160.

21 P. B. Preciado, *Testo Junkie: Sex, Drugs, and Biopolitics in the Pharmacopornographic Era*, trans. B. Benderson (New York: Feminist Press, 2013), 55.

22 J. Rivas, 'Intoxication and Toxicity in a Pharmacopornographic Era: Beatriz Preciado's *Testo Junkie*', paper presented to *Intoxication* conference, Paris, 28 June 2013. The Harry Benjamin International Gender Dysphoria Association was the predecessor of the World Professional Association for Transgender Health.

23 R. Lane, 'Paradigm and Power Shifts in the Gender Clinic', in L. Manderson (ed.), *Technologies of Sexuality, Identity, and Sexual Health* (Abingdon: Routledge, 2012), 205. Whilst Lane believes that more collaborative models of care are emerging, there are still hurdles in terms of equality of access. In cases where healthcare is largely privatized, the conditions trans* people are expected to meet in order to obtain a diagnosis (and therefore treatment) may be somewhat lower. However, both diagnosis and treatment may

by financially inaccessible to most. In countries with public health services, the costs to the individual may be reduced, but there may be delays in treatment, and diagnoses may be made on the basis of more restrictive conditions.

24 Royal College of Psychiatrists, 'Good Practice Guidelines for the Assessment and Treatment of Adults with Gender Dysphoria', *College Report CR181*, October 2013, 21 (http://www.rcpsych.ac.uk/files/pdf version/CR181_Nov15.pdf).

25 Ibid., 25.

26 Preciado, *Testo Junkie*, 348.

27 Ibid., 149.

28 Ibid., 55.

29 Laboria Cuboniks, 'Xenofeminism'.

30 Ibid.

31 Ibid.

32 A. Samuel, 'Why the Future of the Internet May Depend on the History of Abortion', *JSTOR Daily*, 31 May 2016 (https://daily.jstor.org/why-the-future-of-the-internet-may-depend-on-the-history-of-abortion/).

33 Indeed, mesh networks have already proved their usefulness in civil uprisings. The Firechat messaging app, for example – which was originally intended as a way for people to connect whilst off-the-grid at music festivals – has played a role in student-led protests in Taiwan, Hong Kong, and elsewhere. See M. Castillo, 'How a Chat App for Burning Man Turned into a Tool for Revolution', *Adweek*, 25 March 2015 (http://www.adweek.com/digital/how-chat-app-burning-man-turned-tool-revolution-163665).

34 Samuel, 'Why the Future'.

35 Ibid.

36 Ibid.

37 Ibid.

38 Laboria Cuboniks, 'Xenofeminism'.

39 L. Fraser, 'Xenofeminism and New Tactics for the Left', interview with L. Fraser by M. Gerges for *Canadian Art*, 6 February 2017 (http://canadianart.ca/features/xenofeminism).

40 F. Davis, *Moving the Mountain: The Women's Movement in America Since 1960* (Urbana: University of Illinois Press, 1999), 232.

41 Murphy, *Seizing the Means*, 157–8.

42 See Kaplan, *The Story of Jane*, 197.

43 Murphy, *Seizing the Means*, 155.

44 Ibid.

45 Davis, *The Making of Our Bodies, Ourselves*, 201.

46 Ibid.

47 Ibid.

48 Davis, *Moving the Mountain*, 233.

49 Ehrenreich and English, *Complaints and Disorders*, 156–7.

50 Laboria Cuboniks, 'Xenofeminism'.

51 Murphy, *Seizing the Means*, 115–16.

52 Kaplan, *The Story of Jane*, 176.

53 Ibid.

54 Ibid., 176–7.

55 Murphy, *Seizing the Means*, 116.

56 Laboria Cuboniks, 'Xenofeminism'.

57 Murphy, *Seizing the Means*, 28–9.

58 A. R. Galloway and E. Thacker, *The Exploit: A Theory*

NOTES TO PP. 108–17

*of Networks* (Minneapolis: University of Minnesota Press, 2007), 28.
59 Ibid., 29.
60 Ibid.
61 Ibid.
62 Ibid., 30.
63 Ibid., 54.
64 Ibid., 98.
65 Ibid., 100.
66 Davis, *Moving the Mountain*, 234. In 1972, for example, self-help originator Carol Downer was arrested for applying yogurt to a 'patient's' cervix in an attempt to relieve the symptoms of an infection. She was charged with practising medicine without a licence, but was later acquitted.
67 Laboria Cuboniks, 'Xenofeminism'.
68 Murphy, *Seizing the Means*, 161–3.
69 H. Hester, 'Synthetic Genders and the Limits of Micropolitics', . . .*ment Journal*, 2015 (http://journal ment.org/article/synthetic-genders-and-limits-micro politics).
70 A. Corsani, 'Beyond the Myth of Woman: The Becoming-Transfeminist of (Post-)Marxism', *Sub-Stance*, 36(1) (2007), 116.
71 Nelson, *More Than Medicine*, 108.
72 Kaplan, *The Story of Jane*, 45.
73 Ibid.
74 This is not to say that all of these developments lasted into the present day. The feminist health agenda shifted in response to the changing landscape of neoliberalism. Protocols were extended via the

work of NGOs, but the movement's more radical gender-political positions were largely abandoned. Instead, an individualized, depoliticized understanding of health took precedence. Many feminist health facilities were also eventually forced to close owing to financial pressures. See Murphy, *Seizing the Means*.

75 M. Murphy, 'Unsettling Care: Troubling Transnational Itineraries of Care in Feminist Health Practices', *Social Studies of Science*, 45(5) (2015), 3.

76 S. Morgen, *Into Our Own Hands: The Women's Health Movement in the United States, 1969–1990* (New Brunswick, NJ: Rutgers University Press, 2002), 244, n. 3.

77 Davis, *Women, Race and Class*, 204.

78 Ibid.

79 Morgen, *Into Our Own Hands*, 199.

80 Native American people suffering from alcoholism were often provided with Depo-Provera as a means of preventing Fetal Alcohol Syndrome (even in the case of medical contraindications). Rather than seeking to treat the underlying disease, doctors typically preferred to focus on reducing the number of births. See Nelson, *More Than Medicine*.

81 Ehrenreich and English, *Complaints and Disorders*, 158–9.

82 Ibid., 159.

83 Davis, *Women, Race and Class*, 202.

84 Ibid.

85 Ibid., 203.

86 Ibid., 204.

87 Morgen, *Into Our Own Hands*, 244, n. 3.

88 Nelson, *More Than Medicine*, 14.

89 SisterSong, 'What is Reproductive Justice?' n.d. (http://sistersong.net/reproductive-justice/).

90 Ibid.

91 Laboria Cuboniks, 'Xenofeminism'.

92 SisterSong, 'What is Reproductive Justice?'

93 See R. Lipsitz, 'The Pivotal Issue That Pro-Trans Rights Celebrities Remain Oddly Silent About', *Bustle*, 3 May 2016 (https://www.bustle.com/articles/154340-the-pivotal-issue-that-pro-trans-rights-celebrities-remain-oddly-silent-about); K. Pollitt, 'There's a Reason Gay Marriage Is Winning, While Abortion Rights Are Losing', *The Nation*, 22 April 2015 (https://www.thenation.com/article/theres-reason-gay-marriage-winning-while-abortion-rights-are-losing/); J. Michaelson, 'Ten Reasons Women Are Losing While Gays Keep Winning', *The Daily Beast*, 6 July 2014 (http://www.thedailybeast.com/ten-reasons-women-are-losing-while-gays-keep-winning).

94 Nelson, *More Than Medicine*, 57.

95 M. Banzhaf, T. Morgan, and K. Ramspacher, 'Reproductive Rights and AIDS: The Connections', in ACT UP/NY Women and AIDS Book Group (eds), *Women, AIDS and Activism* (Boston: Southend Press, 1992), 204.

96 subRosa, 'Useless Gender', 55–6.

97 One of the only references I can find to the movement engaging with trans* people occurs in Nelson's *More Than Medicine*, which quotes a member of a self-help workshop: 'We had one person who today we would say was transgender, assigned male but now out as

female. It was much more a phenomenon of stretching our understanding by learning about [. . .] gender differences that were not before even a subject to talk about' (95). Whilst trans* issues may have felt alien to this interviewee, it strikes me as odd that recent appraisals of 1970s self-help do so little to address the topic. They tend to be far more sensitive to the pervasive whiteness of the movement than they are to its tacit cissexism.

98 Boston Women's Health Book Collective, 'Afterword: A Message from the Founders of the Boston Women's Health Book Collective', in L. Erickson-Schroth (ed.), *Trans Bodies, Trans Selves: A Resource for the Transgender Community* (Oxford: Oxford University Press, 2014), 592.

99 Ibid.

100 Stryker, *Transgender History*, 146.

101 Ibid.

102 Ibid.

103 L. Porsch, 'Women's Health/Transgender Health: Intersections', in B. Seaman and L. Eldridge (eds), *Voices of the Women's Health Movement: Vol. 1* (New York: Seven Stories Press, 2012), 392.

104 E. Koyama, 'The Transfeminist Manifesto', in R. Dicker and A. Piepmeier (eds), *Catching a Wave: Reclaiming Feminism for the Twenty-First Century* (Boston: Northeastern University Press, 2003), 255.

105 Ibid.

## Conclusion: Xeno-Reproduction

1 See E. Chardronnet, 'GynePunk, the Cyborg Witches of DIY Gynaecology', *Makery*, 30 June 2015 (http:// www . makery . info / en / 2015 / 06 / 30 / gynepunk - les - sorcieres-cyborg-de-la-gynecologie-diy/).

2 D. Bierend, 'Meet the GynePunks Pushing the Boundaries of DIY Gynaecology', *Motherboard*, 21 August 2015 (https://motherboard.vice.com/en_us/ article / qkvyjw / meet - the - gynepunks - pushing - the - boundaries-of-diy-gynecology).

3 K. Oakes, 'GynePunks: A Hacker's Guide to Reimagining Women's Health', *Ob.Gyn. News*, 1 November 2015 (http://www.mdedge.com/obgynnews/ article/103599/gynecology/gynepunks-hackers-guide-reimagining-womens-health).

4 E. D. Thorburn, 'Cyborg Witches: Class Composition and Social Reproduction in the GynePunk Collective', *Feminist Media Studies*, 17(2) (2017), 164.

5 Chardronnet, 'GynePunk'.

6 Thorburn, 'Cyborg Witches', 163.

7 R. Hammond, 'Scientific Strategies Overview', *OSG*, 2016 (http://ryanhammond.us/opensourcegen dercodes_nj.html).

8 R. Hammond, 'Open Source Gendercodes', *OSG*, 2015 (http://opensourcegendercodes.com/projects/osg/).

9 Laboria Cuboniks, 'Xenofeminism'.

10 Ibid.

11 Hammond, 'Open Source Gendercodes'.

12 Laboria Cuboniks, 'Xenofeminism'.